THE
ADOBO ROAD
COOKBOOK

A FILIPINO FOOD JOURNEY—FROM FOOD BLOG, TO FOOD TRUCK, AND BEYOND

MARVIN GAPULTOS

TUTTLE Publishing

Tokyo | Rutland, Vermont | Singapore

CONTENTS

FROM BLOGGER, TO FOOD TRUCKER, TO AUTHOR: MY FILIPINO FOOD JOURNEY

My earliest memories of Filipino food aren't the kind that I fondly recall. It's true that like most Filipino-American kids, I enjoyed eating *lumpia*, *pancit* and garlic-fried rice—the trifecta of crowd-pleasing Filipino food. But my fondness for Filipino food stopped with spring rolls, noodles, and rice. When it came to the dishes my mother loved to cook and my father loved to eat, soulful dishes like *pinakbet*, *adobo*, or *sinigang*, I protested at the dinner table like any reasonable child would—I cried. Loudly.

No, I wanted to eat pizza, and burritos, and hamburgers, and fish sticks (oh, how I loved fish sticks!). I wanted what my friends at school were eating. I wanted the food I saw on television. At the time, as far as I could tell, Magic Johnson drank 7UP, not *calamansi* juice. Punky Brewster shared a plate of pasta with her dog, Brandon, not a plate of *pancit*. And I was certain that Hulk Hogan's mantra of training, saying your prayers, and eating your vitamins had nothing to do with the fermented shrimp paste that my mother claimed would make me a strong boy.

My mother made sure my two brothers and I were fed, even if it meant learning completely new Western dishes to satisfy her young ones' palates. Ever accommodating, she also made sure to cook a separate Filipino dish for her and my father to eat. Otherwise, my dad would have protested like any reasonable grown man would—he surely would have cried. Loudly. Like father, like son, I suppose.

Mind you, these dual dinners didn't last forever. As we got older, my brothers and I gradually began to appreciate Filipino food. However, I didn't fully realize how much I loved my mom's Filipino cooking until I moved away to college. In college, I began to miss the smells of steamed rice and piquant *adobo*—the smells of home that I once ignored and took for granted. Soon enough, the doldrums of dorm food made me see the error of my ways; I had no choice but to eat pizza, and burritos, and hamburgers, and fish sticks (oh, how I detested fish sticks!). So weekend trips back home became more than just a chance to do my laundry for free—those weekends became savored opportunities to eat as much of my mother's cooking as possible.

Despite the rude culinary awakening I experienced in college, it took a few more years, and another change in my life, to trigger a deep, hands-on interest in Filipino food. The trigger? Marriage.

The woman I married isn't a terrible cook. In fact, my wife is a great cook. But it just so happens that my wife isn't Filipino. No matter how delicious a chicken *piccata* my wife could make, it wasn't chicken *adobo*! So whenever I had a sudden urge for some home-cooked Filipino food, we either had to drive a couple of hours to my parents' for dinner, or my cravings simply went unsatisfied.

It wasn't long before I figured out that it would be more convenient to learn how to cook Filipino food on my own, rather than trekking out to my parents' house every week for dinner—besides, my dad might have started charging us for groceries.

So never having cooked a Filipino dish in my entire life, let alone even assisting in the preparation of such a dish (I rarely helped my mom in the kitchen as a kid—I watched cartoons), I set out to learn about the food of my culture. My crash course in Filipino food started with basic questions over the phone to my mother, my grandmother, and my grandmother's sisters ("The Aunties"): "What kind of meat do you use in *lumpia*?", "How long does it take to cook *pinakbet*?", "Will *bagoong* (fermented shrimp paste) kill me?"

When phone calls weren't enough, I found myself in the kitchens of my mom, my grandmother, and my aunties, learning alongside the women of my family who, combined, have hundreds of years of experience honing and perfecting our clan's specific recipes. After much encouragement, I learned to be patient in the kitchen, to trust my instincts and my taste buds, and that no matter how utterly funky a jar of *bagoong* smelled, its contents were indeed safe to eat.

Now armed with the secrets and sage advice of my family, I began cooking and experimenting with Filipino ingredients—to varying degrees of success, of course. And to document my new culinary trials and tribulations, I started the food blog **Burnt Lumpia** (at the time, I was such a novice Filipino cook that I always burned at least one spring roll when making a batch, hence the blog name). What initially began as a means for me to record my recipes, Burnt Lumpia inexplicably became an entertaining distraction for other Internet foodies as more and

TRADITIONAL WAYS ARE WONDERFUL; BUT NEW WAYS, WHEN APPLIED WITH UNDERSTANDING AND SENSITIVITY, CAN CREATE A DISH ANEW—WITHOUT BETRAYING THE TRADITION.

—DOREEN G. FERNANDEZ, FOOD WRITER AND HISTORIAN

more people began reading my blog on a regular basis. I like to think these readers were laughing with me, rather than at me, as I posted stories of my trial-by-fire in Filipino cookery.

As I posted different Filipino recipes on my blog each week, I was ecstatic to find that my readership included not only Filipinos, but readers of different tastes and ethnicities as well. Ultimately, I wanted to urge everyone interested in Filipino food to ask the same questions I did of my family. I wanted people to discover their own family's food traditions and cultures, in the kitchen and at the table, Filipino or otherwise, and celebrate these customs to keep them alive. But I wanted to do more. Eventually, I wanted *everybody* to experience Filipino flavors and ingredients.

But in order to bring a greater awareness and appreciation of Filipino cuisine to the rest of the world, I realized I needed to go beyond blogging. So with my blog recipes in hand, I opened my own Filipino restaurant—well, sort of.

In June of 2010, I opened **The Manila Machine**—Southern California's very first gourmet Filipino food truck. However, The Manila Machine was much more than just a converted taco truck serving Filipino food. It was my own mobile restaurant serving my take on Filipino cuisine. In every sense of the word, the Manila Machine was my personal vehicle for bringing Filipino food to the masses.

Among The Manila Machine's tasty offerings was chicken *adobo*, pork belly and pineapple *adobo*, spicy *sisig*, and *lumpia*. Also made to order were a number of *pan de sal* sliders—bite-sized sandwiches served on traditional Filipino rolls. Not only was I able to successfully field test many of my own recipes, but thousands of Angelenos were also getting their first taste of Filipino food from my mobile kitchen. And they were coming back for more! Soon, people all over Southern California were buzzing about Filipino food, and I was the one feeding them—from a *truck* no less!

At the same time, however, Burnt Lumpia and The Manila Machine both made me realize that there are so many other Filipinos who, like myself, fear losing their own family recipes and simply want to learn more about their own cuisine and culture. I also now know that people of all ethnicities want to

Top: The Manila Machine was Southern California's first gourmet Filipino food truck.

Above: Hungry customers line up for Marvin's take on Filipino cuisine.

enjoy and experience Filipino flavors as much as they do Thai, Vietnamese, and other Asian cuisines.

This shared curiosity in Filipino cuisine, and the need to preserve Filipino culture, is the inspiration for the cookbook you now hold in your hands. This isn't the end-all-be-all Filipino cookbook—far from it. My hope is that this book serves as a starting point that will spark a new and lasting interest in Filipino food and culture.

I want Filipino-American parents to start feeding their toddlers bitter melon so that we can have a new generation of *Pinoys* craving *pinakbet*.

I want college kids to have a freezer bag full of frozen *lumpia*, made by their own hands, so that they can have a mess of crisp spring rolls whenever they please for those late night studying (or drinking) sessions.

I want newlyweds to learn that they must always keep their stash of rice full and at the ready so that they can avoid having to order a pizza when the in-laws pay a surprise visit.

I want Filipinos and non-Filipinos alike to gain a basic understanding of Filipino cuisine so that it can be enjoyed and embraced rather than avoided.

And I want my own children to grow up loving the dishes I cook for them—Filipino food and otherwise.

And that should be a simple enough goal for all of us.

THE NEXT BIG THING?

Today, Filipino food seems to stand at a culinary crossroads. In a world of Twitter, Facebook and food blogs, food-minded people are constantly looking for the next big culinary trend. A hot-button topic within some of these food circles is whether or not Filipino food can be this so-called "next big thing." Alas, the same questions always arise:

"Why isn't Filipino food more popular? Why isn't Filipino food more mainstream?"

Filipino food can be more than simply "trendy"—it is an incredibly diverse and complex cuisine with a multitude of indigenous variations and global influences.

Whether or not Filipino food goes "mainstream" isn't really a concern of mine. For me, in order for Filipino food to be appreciated a little bit more, it must first be understood a little bit more.

With such a diverse culinary heritage and an abundance of nuanced flavors, it's only a matter of time before the rest of the world comes to appreciate and understand Filipino food.

UNDERSTANDING FILIPINO FOOD

The Philippine Archipelago consists of some 7,000 islands clustered in the warm Pacific waters of Southeast Asia. Across these islands, over 100 distinct languages are spoken amongst a multitude of regional ethnicities. And with native cooking techniques such as *adobo* (braising food in vinegar), *kinilaw* (quickly bathing raw food

Adobo, pancit, lumpia, and **shrimp—just a small sampling from a typical meal at my grandmother's home in Delano, CA.**

Left: Harvested rice from my uncle's farm in Badoc, Ilocos Norte, Philippines.

Right: A backyard barbecue in progress at my parents' home in Valencia, CA.

in vinegar or citrus juices), and *ginataan* (cooking food in coconut milk), it is easy to assume that the cuisine of the Philippines consists of an indigenous panoply of Malay-based dishes. But this assumption is only partly true.

There is much more to the story of Filipino cuisine. With a long history as a trading partner with the Chinese, Arabs, Indians, Portuguese and Japanese, the already diverse Malay menu of the Philippines is further accented with flavors and cooking techniques from other parts of the world.

While culinary influences from India, Portugal, and Japan are understated, in certain Filipino dishes, the Muslim influence from Arab trading partners is very apparent in the Muslim region of Mindanao in the southern Philippines.

CHINESE INFLUENCE

Although the Chinese began trading in the Philippines as early as the ninth or tenth centuries, they did not begin to settle in the Philippines in earnest until the sixteenth century. The Chinese influence on Filipino cuisine is most apparent in our *pancit* noodles and *lumpia* spring rolls, but Chinese ingredients such as soy sauce, black beans, tofu, pork and pork lard—just to name a few—have all become mainstays in Filipino cooking.

SPANISH INFLUENCE

The Spanish first arrived in the Philippines in 1521, but would not control the islands until 1565. The Philippines would remain under Spanish rule until 1898. During this 333-year reign, the Spanish would leave an indelible mark on Filipino culture and cuisine.

The Spanish colonists, homesick and hungry, soon began introducing Spanish ingredients, cooking techniques, and dishes to the Philippine natives. Before long, Filipinos began using the Spanish *sofrito* of tomatoes, onions, and garlic cooked in oil as a base to their own dishes, while also embracing and adapting Spanish dishes such as *caldereta*, *empanadas*, *embutido* and *flan*, among many others. And because Spanish ingredients were well beyond the means of many Filipinos at the time, Spanish dishes were reserved for special occasions. Even today, Filipino dishes of Spanish origin are usually only served at birthday parties, graduation parties, and the occasional Manny Pacquiao fight party.

MEXICAN INFLUENCE

Mexico and the Philippines may seem like strange dinner companions, but because both nations were under Spanish rule at the same time, their connection becomes clearer. In fact, during much of its time as a Spanish colony, the Philippines were actually governed indirectly via the Spanish viceroyalty in Mexico City—and this was long before the time of conference calls and telecommuting.

Between the years of 1565–1815, Spain transported goods between its two colonies via the Manila-Acapulco Galleons. These huge ships traveled across the Pacific from Manila to Acapulco only once or twice a year, thereby introducing innumerable Mexican influences into Filipino cuisine. The galleons brought New World crops to the Philippines, such as chocolate, corn, potatoes, tomatoes, pineapples, bell peppers, *jicama*, *chayote*, avocado, peanuts, and annatto—all of which you will find in one form or another in this cookbook. And because the galleons traveled in both directions, the Mexicans received rice, sugarcane, tamarind, coconuts, and mangoes from Philippine soil.

AMERICAN INFLUENCE

Following the end of the Spanish-American War in 1898, Spain signed the Philippines over to the United States as part of the Treaty of Paris. The Philippines would then spend the next half-century as a colony of yet another country and living with a new military force in their presence.

The U.S. military legacy in the Philippines, culinarily speaking, left behind a new fondness for all things American, including things like hot dogs, hamburgers, fried chicken, and ice cream. Even processed convenience foods such as Spam, corned beef, evaporated milk, and instant coffee became highly prized pantry items for the Filipino.

FAMILIAL INFLUENCE

Above all else, Filipino food is largely shaped by individual family traditions and customs. The same dish made in one household will greatly differ from that of the household next door. Taking things a step further, the same dish prepared by one family member will greatly differ from that made by another family member.

This is no more evident than with my own grandmother and her sisters. Even under the same roof and in the same kitchen, each sister prepares her own very distinct version of *adobo*. It is this diversity that makes Filipino cuisine so wonderful.

Speaking of my grandmother and her sisters…

GRANDMA AND "THE AUNTIES," OR MY THREE GRANDMAS

Much of what I know about Filipino food, I learned through a lifetime of visits to the home of my grandparents; Juan and Estrella Gapultos (AKA "Grandpa Johnny" and "Grandma Esther"). Two of my grandmother's sisters, Carolina (AKA "Auntie Carling") and Flora (AKA "Auntie Puyong"), also live in the same household with my grandparents. And although Carling and Puyong are technically my great aunts, I've grown up calling them "Grandma" as well (sorry for all the aliases—Filipino families are "Wu-Tang" like that).

While Grandma Esther does have other siblings, Grandmas Carling and Puyong have lived with my Grandma Esther for my entire life. They are the triumvirate of culinary tutelage with which I was raised—each grandma having her own speciality and excelling at different culinary arts.

My Grandma Esther is definitely the executive chef of her kitchen, directing her (older) sisters in their tasks and orchestrating the many multi-course meals that have fed our family over the decades. With

Grandma Esther and me.

This grandma clan ain't nothin' to mess with. From left to right: Grandma Puyong, Grandma Esther, and Grandma Carling.

a degree in Home Economics from the University of the Philippines, my Grandma Esther is an all-around great cook, though her specialty is in desserts. As such, in addition to my grandmother being an expert in traditional Filipino sweets, she's also adept at baking everything from multi-tiered wedding cakes decorated with ornate sugar flowers, to mini pecan tartlets.

Grandmas Carling and Puyong, on the other hand, both specialize in the old school: traditional Filipino fare from the Northern Ilocos region of the Philippines. Most every Filipino comfort food from my childhood has been prepared by either Grandma Carling or Grandma Puyong. I imagine if there were ever any sort of "Filipino Throwdown" or "Iron Chef Philippines" competition, those two young ladies would wipe the floor with whoever crossed them.

And although my three grandmas sometimes bicker amongst themselves in the kitchen (as all sisters do), they always manage to create beautiful, soulful meals together.

In fact, if I could choose my last meal on earth, it would consist of delicacies described in this book: my Grandma Carling's Pancit Miki (page 58), my Grandma Puyong's Pinakbet (page 49), and my Grandma Esther's Buchi (page 130).

EAT LIKE A FILIPINO

Although this cookbook is broken down into convenient sections that focus on different Filipino "courses," it should be noted that, typically, Filipinos do not eat meals that progress from small plates, to main courses, to dessert. Instead, all courses are brought to the table and presented at the same time—desserts included.

Now this doesn't mean that we'll have a bite of cake sandwiched between nibbles of spring roll, slurps of soup, and mouthfuls of roast pork (though, admittedly, I've done that once or twice at family parties, but I digress), but rather, it signifies the importance of food to a Filipino family. Feeding, being fed, and sharing in a meal is vital to all cultures—but especially so with Filipinos.

If you've ever eaten a Filipino meal with a Filipino family, you probably know that one of the most difficult things is trying to get up from the dinner table—not only because you are full of food, but also because the host is likely to insist that you keep eating some more! And even if you do manage to escape the dinner table, chances are that you will be bringing more food home with you in doggie bags. Filipino food: the gift that keeps on giving.

AN ABUNDANCE OF RICE

Central to any Filipino meal is the appearance of rice at the table. Rice is served with all meals throughout the day. For breakfast, fried rice (Fast and Simple Garlic Fried Rice page—53) is often served alongside eggs and sausage, or a warm *champorado* (Chocolate and Coffee Rice Pudding, page 135) can also be had for breakfast. Steamed white rice, of course, is ubiquitous for lunch and dinner and serves as an absorber of soups and stews, or as a bed for protein and vegetables, or as a blank canvas for various dips, sauces and condiments. Rice even appears in many Filipino desserts, either in its sticky glutinous form for heavy sweet snacks, or when milled into rice flour to form the foundation of many cakes and dumplings.

A TRADITION OF SOURNESS

As you'll find throughout the recipes in this book, the most dominant flavor in Filipino food is sourness. This sourness can be a quick zing provided from anything like a dipping sauce made of fresh *calamansi* lime juice, or it can be a more restrained and refined sourness that can be found in *adobos* slowly simmered in vinegar and spices (page 68).

The Filipino penchant for lip-puckering zest is not without reason. In the tropical climes of the Philippines, the preservative powers of vinegar were a culinary necessity for centuries, long before refrigeration was available.

Also arising from this tropical climate was an abundance of fruit and vegetables ripe with tang. Aside from the citrus bite of *calamansi*, sourness was also sought out in green mangoes, tamarind, guavas, and a variety of other exotic produce.

As such, throughout the ages the collective taste of Filipinos has centered around sourness.

But to think that *all* Filipino food is sour would be a great underestimation. Filipino cuisine is rich in all flavors of the palate.

SAVOR EVERYTHING, WASTE NOTHING

While "nose-to-tail" eating may be somewhat of a hot trend in high-end restaurants these days, Filipinos (along with many other cultures) have long appreciated the virtues of eating whole-hog.

There are a variety of wonderfully delicious Filipino dishes in which organ meats and other "scrap" bits are used and highlighted. The Filipino use of offal is one of cultural tradition that occurred before, during, and after colonial times and still continues today. This tradition of enjoying every last bit of an animal arises not only out of thrift or necessity, but because these bits taste darn good.

Throughout this cookbook, I do provide a small sampling of such recipes to perhaps whet your beak with "real-deal" delicacies ranging from chicken feet and livers, to salmon heads, to various tasty bits of pork. These tasty bits will open a whole new delicious world of flavors and textures.

Savor them. Enjoy them.

ABOUT THE RECIPES

You'll notice that with many of the English recipe titles throughout this book, I also provide a Filipino translation. I realize that with over 120 languages (and several hundred dialects), there is more than one way to refer to a dish. As a general rule, I tried to stick with the more common Tagalog dialect for easier identification among my Filipino readers. But there are a few instances in which I use the Ilocano terminology for a dish. In these cases, the specific dish may be one from my childhood that I learned from my grandmother, aunties, and mother.

As I mentioned earlier, my culinary viewpoint largely stems from my American upbringing in an Ilocano family originating from the Northern Philippines. With that said, I also have a unique culinary disposition from years of developing recipes for a blog read by an international audience, as well as developing recipes for a successful Filipino food truck whose customer base was the multi-ethnic hodgepodge of Los Angeles, California.

As such, the recipes I provide in this book are easy-to-follow, tried-and-true recipes that can serve as a basic guide to the pleasures of Filipino cuisine, authentic dishes that can easily be enjoyed by Filipinos and non-Filipinos alike.

But in addition to some classic and traditional recipes, I've also (ahem) taken some liberties with my own "new school" interpretations. These new adaptations are not meant to dilute Filipino tastes. Rather, they are creative steps in the continuing evolution of a vital cuisine, taking advantage of traditional flavors and ingredients to spark a new interest in Filipino food and culture.

Mabuhay!

Marvin Gapultos
www.BurntLumpiaBlog.com

SOME USEFUL TOOLS

In all honesty, you don't need any fancy cooking gadgets to make great Filipino food. Because of the many different ethnic influences on Filipino food, and because of the large diaspora of Filipinos living in other countries, Filipino cooking is naturally adaptable to any kitchen. Step inside the kitchen of most any Filipino grandmother and you may notice only a pot or two, some knives, and a wooden spoon (not counting the kitschy one hanging on the wall). With that said, here is a list of the few tools needed to outfit your burgeoning Filipino kitchen—a kitchen that would make any Filipino grandmother proud, or very jealous.

BOX GRATER: A simple yet durable four sided stainless steel grater can go a long way in the kitchen. Aside from grating cheese, I also use my handy box grater for shredding any number of fruits and vegetables needed to be mixed into various Filipino dishes such as *lumpia*, *pancit*, *atchara* and the like.

COCKTAIL SHAKER: As you'll see in Chapter 6, "Filipino Finger Foods and Cocktails," there is a rich history of cocktails in Filipino cuisine. As such, a good sturdy cocktail shaker is a handy and necessary tool when mixing a number of different drinks. The shaker made by OXO is a good all-around cocktail shaker that doesn't leak and has plenty of room for liquids and ice.

DEEP FRY THERMOMETER: Filipino cuisine has more than its fair share of deep-fried delicacies. Although there are other ways of checking oil temperature (e.g. dropping a cooked rice grain into the oil to see if it sizzles), a deep fry thermometer takes the guesswork out of frying and allows you to better control and maintain the desired frying temperature. It's also inexpensive and easy to store—more reasons why you should own one.

FINE-MESH SIEVE/STRAINER: An indispensable tool for straining stocks as well as for draining any number of fragile Filipino noodles. Choose a large metal sieve that will still fit into your largest bowl.

KNIVES: You don't need an entire set of expensive knives to be a good cook. I know it may seem like common sense in today's world of cooking shows and food blogs, but I'll say it anyway: you only need one good chef's knife. My personal knife of choice is the Shun Ken Onion Chef's Knife. It cuts like a dream and feels like it was custom fitted to my hand. I use my Shun for everything from breaking down whole chickens, to portioning precise squares of pork belly, and my favorite—smashing cloves of garlic. But I suggest you use whatever knife is comfortable in your own hand, making sure that the knife you choose remains sharpened and honed at all times. A sharp knife is a safe knife, and a safe knife is a versatile knife.

NONREACTIVE COOKWARE: Because acidic liquids, such as vinegar and citrus juices, are used so frequently in Filipino cuisine, it's vitally important that you use nonreactive cookware such as stainless steel or enameled cast iron. Do not use aluminum cookware as it will color acidic foods with a gray tinge. Do not

Box grater

Cocktail shaker

Fine-mesh sieve/strainer

Knives

Nonreactive cookware

Oven-safe ramekins

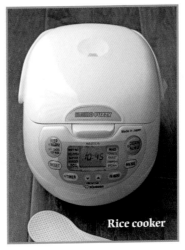

Rice cooker

Roasting pan

use cast iron (enameled cast iron is okay) as acidic foods will leach iron from the pan. The pots and pans I used the most while writing this cookbook were a large stainless steel sauté pan for searing meats and stir-frying vegetables, and a 6-quart enameled Dutch oven for making soups, stocks, and many *adobos*.

OVEN-SAFE RAMEKINS:

Ramekins can be used for so much more than for just holding prepped vegetables (does anyone really use ramekins for that anyway?). Ramekins with a capacity of 6–8 ounces are perfect for making individual dessert servings like Creamy Leche Flan Custard (page 138), or for more savory applications like pot pies.

RICE COOKER: Plain and simple,

an electric rice cooker is an essential tool for every Asian household, or even any household that prepares Asian food on a regular basis. I've lived my entire life with a rice cooker in

my home—*literally*—so I don't know how I'd function without one. My current rice cooker of choice is the Zojirushi Neuro Fuzzy model, where "Neuro Fuzzy" is just some techie-speak for "this rice cooker does a bunch of other stuff besides cooking rice." For instance, I often set the timer of my rice cooker so that a batch of warm oatmeal is ready for me when I come downstairs in the morning. The Zojirushi is an investment, but in return you'll have perfectly cooked rice, among other things, whenever you want. While the fancy Zojirushi is nice to have, you can definitely get by with a more inexpensive rice cooker. In fact, I owned a tiny 3-cup capacity one-button rice cooker throughout college, through my days as a bachelor, and into my first years of marriage. That's a long stretch of time for a "cheapo" rice cooker.

ROASTING PAN: A large heavy

roasting pan is not only useful for roasting big hunks of meat or large amounts of vegetables,

but it is also a great vessel for making the water bath necessary for a creamy *leche flan*. Choose a roasting pan that has handles you can comfortably grab while you have oven mitts on your hands.

SPIDER SKIMMER: Primarily

used for fetching fried items from hot oil, a bamboo spider skimmer with a steel mesh basket is also great for draining small amounts of noodles and blanched vegetables, or plucking hard-boiled eggs from boiling water.

WOK: Like the Chinese, Filipinos

use the wok (called a *kawali* in the Philippines) for deep-frying, stir-frying, and steaming. Large 14-inch carbon steel woks with a flat bottom are not only inexpensive, but they are the perfect shape for most home stovetops. Choose a wok with a long heatproof handle on one side, and a shorter helper handle on the other side. Also be sure that you have a metal wok spatula that is specially shaped to fit the curves of your wok to better flip and stir food during cooking.

Spider skimmer

Wok

STOCKING YOUR FILIPINO PANTRY

One of the stumbling blocks to cooking a great Filipino meal is the perceived lack of available Filipino ingredients. But considering the fact that Filipino cuisine is heavily influenced by the cuisines of China, Spain, Mexico, and the U.S., and because Filipino cuisine shares many similar ingredients to other Southeast Asian countries like Vietnam and Thailand, it is very likely that you'll be able to find the ingredients you need without traveling too far from your home. With the proliferation of large Latin and Asian markets, as well as smaller markets that specifically cater to Southeast Asians, the world of Filipino food is more accessible now than ever before.

While I'm fortunate enough to live near a large Asian grocery store, as well as a small Filipino market, I can usually find many ingredients in my local supermarket as well. So even if you live in a small town without any ethnic markets, it is still possible to find all the ingredients you need from the ethnic foods aisle at your regular grocery store, or by ordering more hard-to-find items from the internet.

The following is a list of the Filipino ingredients I use most often; the same ingredients I relied upon to write this book. This isn't a conclusive list that will turn your kitchen into Little Manila, but it is a list to get you well on your way to preparing dozens of Filipino dishes.

ANNATTO SEEDS (ACHUETE): Part of the legacy from the Manila-Acapulco galleon trade, annatto seeds are usually steeped in cooking oil to produce annatto oil (see page 26). The annatto oil is then used to impart a beautiful—and natural—reddish-orange hue to any number of dishes.

BANANA KETCHUP/SAUCE: A sweeter, fruitier version of tomato ketchup, banana ketchup is, indeed, made from bananas. A popular condiment in the Philippines, banana ketchup is used as a dip for fries and a topping for burgers, but is also used with grilled meats and is a primary ingredient in Filipino Spaghetti (page 64). Artificially dyed a bright red hue to resemble tomato ketchup, banana ketchup can be easily found in Asian markets and in the Ethnic aisle of some supermarkets, but an all-natural and delicious version can be easily made at home (see page 24).

BANANA LEAVES: The large, pliable leaves of the banana tree are used for wrapping any number of steamed, grilled, or baked food items. The banana leaf not only makes for a great cooking vessel and "to-go" wrapper, but it also imbues a fragrant grassy aroma to whatever food is held inside.

BAY LEAVES: One of the primary ingredients in *adobos* (page 68), it is also known as "laurel," and imparts a depth of warmth and flavor with subtle woody and floral notes. Either dried or fresh bay leaves can be used, though the dried variety tends to have a stronger aroma and flavor than the fresh variety.

BITTER MELON (AMPALAYA): Also known as

bitter gourd, are pale green in color with an irregular wrinkly surface and are, indeed, quite bitter in flavor. Bitter melons are reputed to have an abundance of health benefits and are used in dishes throughout the Philippines, though they are mostly used in the northern part of the archipelago.

BOK CHOY: A mild Chinese cabbage, it is favored in Filipino cooking because of its crunchy texture and versatility. And because it cooks so quickly, *bok choy* can be added at the last moment to stir-fries and soups to add crunch and a vibrant green color.

CASSAVA (KAMOTENG KAHOY): *Cassava* (also known as *yucca* or *manioc*) is a large tuber native to South America. Because of its very high starch content, *cassava* is primarily used in desserts and cakes in Filipino cuisine.

CHAYOTE (SAYOTE): *Chayote* (also known as *mirliton*) is a green pear-shaped squash with a large single seed in the center. *Chayote* is mild in flavor but retains a firm

CALAMANSI: *Calamansi* limes (also *kalamansi* or *calmondin*) are small citrus fruits that have the fragrance of mandarin oranges and the sour citrus flavor of lemons and limes. *Calamansi* limes are about 1 inch (2.5 cm) in diameter and range in color from green to orange. A squeeze, a squirt, or a spritz of *calamansi* nectar brightens up any dish—from noodles, to soups, to grilled meats and fish. *Calamansi*

juice is also great when mixed into desserts and cocktails as well. *Calamansi* can sometimes be found at Asian markets or even at local farmers' markets, so if you ever encounter these fragrant orbs, be sure to buy in bulk! I've found that 1 lb (500 g) of *calamansi* limes often yields between ¾ cup (185 ml) to 1 cup (250 ml) of juice. But the best way to ensure a steady supply of these wonderful limes is to grow your own tree in your back yard. Potted *calamansi* trees can often be found in the nursery department of hardware stores, and the small potted trees can be purchased online as well. And of course, fresh lemon juice or lime juice can always be substituted for *calamansi*.

texture even when cooked, so it is often used in soups and stews in Filipino cuisine.

COCONUT MILK: Coconut milk is made from the shredded flesh of mature brown coconuts that is mixed with water and pressed. Coconut milk made from the first pressing is thicker and richer, while subsequent pressings produce thinner and less flavorful coconut milk. Although freshly made coconut milk is preferred in the Philippines, canned unsweetened coconut milk can be used with equally wonderful results. I prefer the Chaokoh and Arroy-D brands of canned coconut milk from Thailand, as they both are consistently flavorful and creamy. When working with canned coconut milk, always give the can a vigorous shake before opening, and then after opening the can, use a spoon to stir the coconut milk again before adding it to your dish.

DRIED RED PEPPER FLAKES: I use these spicy flakes to add a hint of heat to dishes when I don't have fresh chili peppers on hand—though sometimes I use both at the same time to achieve different layers of spice.

EDAM CHEESE: Believe it or not, Edam cheese is a common ingredient in Filipino cuisine. Spheres of the Dutch cheese covered in red wax are traditionally given as Christmas gifts in the Philippines. The savory cheese is often grated onto many Filipino desserts as a salty counterpoint. Keep in mind that the Edam found in Asian markets is usually specifically marketed towards Filipinos and therefore tends to be saltier than Edam found in other grocery stores. Gouda makes a great substitute if you can't find Edam.

EVAPORATED MILK: A convenience food introduced by the Americans, evaporated milk is milk that is boiled and processed until it has lost about half of its water content and then canned and sterilized. Canned evaporated milk is used primarily in Filipino desserts.

FERMENTED BLACK BEANS: Also known as Chinese dried black beans, these salty beans are made from fermented black soybeans and are used to season soups, stews, meats, and poultry. They can be found in Asian markets and are usually sold in plastic bags or cardboard containers. I prefer the Yang Jiang brand in a plastic bag.

FERMENTED FISH/SHRIMP PASTE [BAGOONG]: A very pungent and salty condiment that can be made from tiny fish or tiny shrimp. *Bagoong alamang* (also labeled as shrimp fry) is perhaps the most commonly available type of shrimp paste available in the States, and is often sautéed with garlic and shallots (page 26) and used as a condiment to enhance any number of dishes that need a salty kick.

FISH SAUCE [PATIS]: Ubiquitous throughout Southeast Asia, fish sauce is an essential ingredient in Filipino cooking and is used not only to impart saltiness, but savoriness (*umami*) as well. Fish sauce is made from fermented anchovies. Although it has a very pungent aroma, if used properly it will not make your food taste "fishy." Fish sauce can be used to season cooked dishes, but it can also be used as part of a dipping sauce (page 27). Shop for fish sauce that is light amber in color and labeled as being made from the first extraction of the fish. Keep in mind that the saltiness in fish sauce varies by brand. Rufina is a good brand of Filipino fish sauce, but Three Crabs (Vietnam), Red Boat (Vietnam) and Squid (Thailand) are also very good brands of fish sauce.

GINGER [LUYA]: A rhizome rather than a root, ginger imparts a bright, sweet, zesty, and spicy flavor that I love to put into nearly everything I cook. When shopping for ginger, look for smooth and tight skin without any blemishes. Ginger with wrinkles tend to be older and more fibrous.

GREEN MANGO: Green mangoes are simply firm, unripe mangoes prized for their sour flavor. Usually sliced and served with *bagoong* for a salty-sour snack, green mangoes can also provide texture and tartness to raw salads. Look for green mangoes that are very firm and have a pale green skin. You can find green mangoes in Asian markets.

GREEN PAPAYA: Green papayas are simply unripe papayas that are mild in flavor rather than sweet. Green papayas have dark green skins with a firm white flesh and a cluster of seeds in the middle of the fruit. Green papaya is often pickled (page 22) but it is also used in a variety of Filipino soups.

JICAMA [SINKAMAS]: A South American tuber, *jicama* is round with brown skin and white flesh. Because of its crispy texture, *jicama* is often eaten raw in salads, or even sliced like an apple and dipped in *bagoong*. I like to use *jicama* with smooth brown skins and that are no larger than the size of a softball as they tend to be easier to prep and slice.

KABOCHA SQUASH [KALABASA]: A sweetish winter squash from Japan, *kabocha* are shaped like small pumpkins and have a dark green knobby skin with orange or yellow flesh. Commonly sold in 2–3 pound (1–1.5 kg) sizes in the supermarket, this squash is often used in soups and stews in the Philippines.

LEMONGRASS [TANGLAD]: Lemongrass is an aromatic and edible species of grass that lends a beautiful lemon flavor and aroma without any acid. The whole length of a lemongrass stalk provides aroma, but only the tender bottom portion of the stalk is edible.

LONG BEANS [SITAO]: Also called Chinese long beans, snake beans, or yard-long beans, long beans are indeed long green beans that usually measure 2–3 feet in length. Long beans are easy to find in the produce section in many Asian markets and are usually bundled together in bunches. Look for bright green specimens without any blemishes. Tender green beans are a suitable substitute for long beans.

MACAPUNO: Because of a natural occurring mutation, *macapuno* coconuts lack the water usually found at the center of regular coconuts. Instead, *macapuno* coconuts are solid throughout with a sweet jellylike flesh. *Macapuno* flesh is usually shredded, preserved in sugar syrup and packed in glass jars. Jars of *macapuno* can be found at Asian markets and labeled as "*Macapuno* Strings" or "Coconut Sport." And because of the *natural* mutation of the coconut, don't be alarmed if the label on a *macapuno* jar also reads "Mutant Coconut."

MANGO: Ask any Filipino what their favorite fruit is and they are likely to say, "mangoes." Although unripe green mangoes (page 16) are prized for their sourness in the Philippines, soft ripe mangoes are beloved and even lusted for in the Philippines. I've heard many arguments from Filipinos that ripe Philippine-grown mangoes are superior to any other mangoes from around the world. After having tasted a sweet, custardy mango in the Philippines myself, I have to agree. Philippine mangoes are incredibly smooth and are nearly devoid of any stringy fibers so prevalent in other mango varieties. Unfortu-

nately, the mangoes labeled as "Manila Mangoes" sold here in the States are often actually grown in Mexico. Despite this misleading nomenclature, you can still find a great variety of mangoes in many grocery stores. When choosing mangoes, look for fruits with smooth taut skin. When ripe, the mango should feel heavy for its size, and it should smell sweet and deeply fruity. Lastly, give the mango a squeeze—it should be slightly soft and yield a bit to your fingertips.

MISO: A Japanese ingredient made of fermented soybeans, *miso* is often used to add flavor and savoriness to Filipino soups. *Miso* paste comes in a variety of shades and colors, with lighter shades being mild in flavor and darker shades being more robust. *Miso* can be found in the refrigerated section (usually right next to the *tofu*) at Asian markets and most large supermarkets.

MUNG BEANS [MONGGO]: Dried *mung* beans are used in a variety of ways in Filipino cooking. They are often ground and made into *mung* bean noodles (*sotanghon*), or cooked and sweetened for use in desserts, and also simmered to make hearty stews (page 55).

PANCIT NOODLES: There are as many types of *pancit* noodles as there are ways to prepare them. Here are the *pancit* noodles used in this cookbook:

Chinese-Style Wheat Noodles (*Pancit Canton*): *Pancit canton* are dried yellow noodles made from wheat flour, oil, and salt. They cook quickly, and are great in stir-fries.

Fresh Wheat Noodles (*Pancit Miki*): Unlike many other types of *pancit* noodles, *pancit miki* are often sold fresh in the refrigerated section of Asian markets. They are made simply from wheat, water and artificial colors, though I do provide a homemade version in this cookbook (page 58).

Mung Bean Thread Noodles (*Pancit Sotanghon*): *Pancit sotanghon*, also known as

bean thread, or vermicelli noodles are dried noodles made from *mung* bean starch and water. Before cooking with them, these noodles must be soaked in very hot water until they become soft and translucent.

RICE FLOUR AND GLUTINOUS RICE FLOUR: Regular rice flour is made from milled long-grain rice and is very fine and light in texture. Rice flour is used to make a variety of desserts and dumplings in Filipino cuisine. My grandmother uses a Thai brand of rice flour called Erawan that can be found in Asian markets. I prefer this brand as well. Glutinous rice flour (also labeled as "sweet rice flour") is milled from short-grain glutinous rice. Glutinous rice flour is also very fine and light and used in many desserts and dumplings. Again, the Erawan brand is preferred, but the Mochiko brand of sweet rice flour can also be used, though it is not as finely textured as the Erawan brand. For certain recipes, both rice flour and glutinous rice flour are used in tandem to affect the final texture of the dish.

SALT: The Philippines has its own variety of artisanal and locally harvested sea salts that rival those produced in other parts of the world. You can find gourmet Philippine sea salts in many upscale markets and from online retailers. Though I do love to use a fine-grained Philippine sea salt in my cooking, I often use kosher salt interchangeably with my Filipino sea salt.

SAMBAL OELEK: Though not a traditional ingredient in Filipino cuisine, I do love using this spicy chili paste in marinades because it easily mixes into liquids and provides a convenient form of heat and spice. *Sambal oelek* chili paste can be found in small plastic jars in Asian markets, as well as in some supermarkets—either in the Ethnic aisle or right next to other commercially prepared hot sauces.

SHALLOTS: An aromatic bulb that is similar to an onion, but smaller in size and milder in flavor, shallots are used raw or sautéed along with garlic and ginger in many Filipino recipes.

SMOKED SPANISH PAPRIKA (PIMENTÓN): Made from ground chili peppers that are first dried and smoked over oak fires, smoked Spanish paprika lends a wonderfully rich and smoky flavor and aroma when sprinkled onto meats, poultry, and fish. It can be found in the spice aisle of most grocery stores, and it can also be ordered online.

STICKY RICE (MALAGKIT): Not to be confused with everyday long or short-grained rice, sticky rice is primarily used in desserts and snacks in the Philippines. Also known as glutinous rice or sweet rice, sticky rice has a higher starch content than regular rice and therefore becomes more sticky and chewy when cooked—hence its name. Regular white sticky rice can be found in Asian markets right next to other rice varieties, so be careful when reading the labels. In addition, a number of heirloom rice varieties grown in the Philippines are

now becoming available in gourmet markets and from online retailers, so these are worth seeking out as well.

SOY SAUCE (TOYO): Introduced to the Philippines by Chinese traders, soy sauce is used as a dipping sauce as well as a seasoning to cooked dishes. I prefer to use the low sodium variety of the Kikkoman brand in my everyday cooking.

TARO (GABI): A tropical root vegetable valued for its starchy tuber, *taro* must be cooked to reduce its inherent toxicity prior to

consumption. *Taro* root imparts a nutty-sweet flavor to dishes, and is used in soups such as *sinigang* (page 62). *Taro* leaves provide the greens for *laing* (page 46).

THAI CHILI PEPPERS (SILING LABUYO): Also known as Thai bird or bird's eye chili peppers, these small fiery pods are the spice of choice in the Philippines. They can be thinly sliced and tossed raw into dipping sauces, or added to cooked dishes for extra

TAMARIND: The green unripe variety of tamarind pods is primarily used as a souring agent in Filipino cuisine—especially in the sour soup known as *Sinigang*. The most accessible forms of tamarind, though, can be found in Asian markets either in blocks of pulp, jarred as concentrate, or in packets of artificially flavored powder. Because of its artificial flavors and preservatives, I tend to stay away from the powdered tamarind (though many Filipino home cooks use them in a pinch). The jarred tamarind concentrate consists of only water and tamarind and is the easiest to use—just pour the contents out. To use the blocks of tamarind, soak 3 oz (75 g) of the tamarind pulp in 1 cup (250 ml) of hot water for a few minutes, and then strain out the seeds and pulp and use the tamarind water in the recipe.

spice. Thai chili peppers are also often pickled (page 20).

VINEGAR (SUKA): Vinegar is perhaps the most used (and thereby important) ingredient in the Filipino kitchen, due in large part to the extended shelf life bestowed upon food cooked in vinegar—a necessary culinary "voodoo" needed for tropical climes during the days before refrigeration. But aside from its preservative powers, vinegar is also used simply because an element of sourness is the most prevalent (and preferred) flavor in Filipino cuisine. For instance, vinegar is the key player in many Filipino dishes like *paksiw, kinilaw* (page 36), various dipping sauces, and a variety of different marinades. And of course, *adobo* (page 68) is perhaps the prime example of a vinegar-based Filipino dish.

In the Philippines, a variety of locally sourced, artisanal vinegars are made from the fermented nectar, sap, or juices found in different plants or fruits grown in the surrounding areas. Luckily, many of these vinegars can be found at Asian markets. Datu Puti, Tropics, and Masagana are all good brands from the Philippines.

The vinegars I list here generally hover between 4–5 percent acidity. And while each of them provide different nuanced flavors, they can generally be substituted for each other in the recipes of this cookbook. Also, for each recipe that uses a Filipino vinegar, I do provide a more accessible alternate (e.g. apple cider vinegar, white distilled vinegar, unseasoned rice vinegar).

Palm Vinegar (*Sukang Paombong*): Filipino Palm Vinegar is made from the fermented sap of the *nipa* palm. It is named for the region of the Philippines that is known for its Palm Vinegar—Paombong. *Sukang paombong* is cloudy white in appearance and has subtle notes of lemon and citrus.

Coconut Vinegar (*Sukang Tuba*): Filipino coconut sap vinegar is made from the fermented sap of a coconut tree and is perhaps the most used vinegar in the Philippines due to the abundance of coconuts. *Sukang tuba* is also cloudy white in appearance, with a slightly sweet smell. Despite its provenance, coconut vinegar lacks any coconut flavor or aroma, but is instead very pungent and sour. In addition to finding coconut vinegar in Asian markets, organic varieties of coconut vinegar can also be found (for a higher price) in health food stores.

Dark Sugarcane Vinegar (*Sukang Iloco*): Filipino cane vinegar from the Ilocos region of the Philippines is a by-product of Ilocano sugarcane wine known as *basi*. *Basi* is made by pressing juice from the sugarcane, cooking the juice to a thick molasses state, and then placing the molasses in clay jars. The bark from the *duhat* (Java plum) tree is then added to the clay jars as a flavoring and fermenting agent. The molasses first turns into the alcoholic *basi* wine, but if left to ferment longer and sour, the *basi* then transforms to *sukang iloco*. *Sukang iloco* is dark brown in color and somewhat mellow in flavor, though it does have a hint of sweetness to it. Although Ilocano cane vinegar can be used in a wide variety of applications, I find it best when used in Ilocano foods such as *longganisa* (page 93) and *empanadas* (page 34). When *sukang iloco* is used in cooked dishes, such as an *adobo* (page 68), the final dish will have a very subtle sweet aftertaste.

White Sugarcane Vinegar (*Sukang Maasim*): White sugarcane vinegar is made from fermented sugarcane syrup. Sugarcane is first pressed for its juice and sap, and then the juice and sap are cooked and left to ferment into vinegar. *Sukang maasim* is only slightly cloudy, almost clear, and is relatively mild in flavor. It is an all-purpose vinegar good for use in everything from *adobo* to dipping sauces.

WRAPPERS: With a variety of styles of *lumpia* available in Filipino cuisine, it might be difficult trying to decide on which wrapper to purchase when rolling your Filipino spring rolls. Here are two readily available wrappers that will produce crisp *lumpia* with smooth skins:

Lumpia Wrappers: Filipino *lumpia* wrappers are thin, nearly translucent round skins made from wheat flour, water, oil, and salt. They are most commonly sold in sizes of 9–10 in (23–25 cm) in diameter in the frozen foods section of Asian markets. They should be completely thawed before use. When fried, *lumpia* wrappers remain smooth and crisp rather than having any bubbles in the skin. The Tropics brand of *lumpia* wrappers is a good choice.

Spring Roll Wrappers: Square spring roll wrappers can be used in place of round *lumpia* wrappers. Spring roll wrappers are similar to *lumpia* wrappers in that they are also comprised of wheat flour, water, oil, and salt. And also like *lumpia* wrappers, spring roll wrappers are super thin and fry up smooth and crisp. However, spring roll wrappers are usually sold in 8-in (20-cm) squares, rather than rounds. I actually prefer using square spring roll wrappers when rolling *lumpia* because I find the square shape slightly easier to work with. I prefer the Spring Home brand of spring roll wrappers—they are usually sold frozen in packages of 25.

THE BASICS

The simple recipes in this section will go a long way toward providing a solid foundation of delightful flavors for your Filipino meals. The savory stocks create the base essence for a variety of soup and noodle dishes, providing the richness of shrimp or chicken to whatever recipe they are stirred into. And because no Filipino meal is complete without a table-side selection of *sawsawan* (the *Pinoy* term for dipping sauces), the variety of condiments, sauces, and dips described here will taste worlds better than any of the relatively expensive commercially prepared offerings that you could purchase in an Asian market. Everything, from basic sauces of soy and citrus, to homemade banana ketchup, annatto oil, pickles, and mayonnaise, will enable you and your family to further customize and tinker with the already flavorful Filipino dishes you bring to the table.

SPICY PICKLED PEPPERS SUKANG SILI

Pickled Thai chili peppers are a common Filipino condiment. The very spicy preserved peppers can be eaten whole, but they are usually chopped and served with the spicy vinegar in which they were steeped. This fiery chili vinegar is commonly known as *sukang sili*, and it is usually paired with fried or grilled foods.

This recipe is for use in a 16-oz (500-ml) glass jar. If using a larger container, or if you simply want to double the recipe, first place the chili peppers into the empty container, pour in enough water to cover, and then pour this water out into a measuring cup. The amount of water in the measuring cup will be the amount of vinegar you need to pickle the peppers. For each cup of vinegar, I like to add 2 teaspoons of salt and 2 teaspoons of sugar, but you can adjust this to your own tastes. Feel free to use any type of chili pepper in this recipe, adjusting the size of your jar or container accordingly.

Makes 16 oz (500 ml)
Prep Time: 5 minutes
Cooking Time: 10 minutes

¼ lb (100 g) Thai chili peppers, washed and stems trimmed
1 cup (250 ml) white Filipino cane vinegar, or white distilled vinegar, plus more if needed
1 bay leaf
1 teaspoon whole black peppercorns
¼ teaspoon dried red pepper flakes
2 teaspoons sugar, plus more if needed
2 teaspoons salt, plus more if needed

Pierce each pepper with a paring knife—this will allow the vinegar to seep into the chili peppers more quickly. Place the chili peppers into a clean glass pint jar, or other nonreactive container with an airtight lid.

Combine the rest of the ingredients in a small saucepan over high heat. Bring to a boil, and then cover and simmer over low heat for 5 minutes. Remove the pickling liquid from the heat and pour it over the chili peppers in the jar. Screw the lid onto the jar and cool to room temperature. Once cool, store the chili peppers in the refrigerator.

As the chili peppers settle and absorb the vinegar, you may find that there is additional space in the jar. If this is the case, you can add more fresh vinegar to the jar to top it off. Store the jar in the refrigerator for at least a few days before using. The chili peppers will keep in the refrigerator for at least 3 weeks.

COOK'S NOTE: Besides using these pickled peppers and spicy vinegar as a condiment, try using them in my Bloody Mario cocktail (page 119).

SHRIMP STOCK

Asians have long known that an amazing amount of flavor can be found in the heads and shells of shrimp. Filipinos in particular love cooking head-on, shell-on shrimp and then gleefully sucking the juices from the shrimp head. So it's a shame that such flavorful fodder often goes unused. My grandmother makes her shrimp stock by pounding the heads and shells in a bowl with a spoon and then mixing the extracted "juice" with some water. But I find my mother's method of blitzing everything in a blender much easier. Although peeling and deveining shrimp can be tedious, it's worth it considering that a good amount of rich stock can be made from a small of amount of shrimp heads and shells.

Makes about 8 cups (about 1.75 liters)
Prep Time: 30 minutes
Cooking Time: 30 minutes

1 lb (500 g) raw, head-on, shell-on, medium shrimp
3 cloves garlic, smashed with the side of a knife and peeled
2 bay leaves
1 teaspoon whole black peppercorns
8 cups (1.75 liters) water

Peel and devein the shrimp, adding the shrimp heads and shells to a large pot and reserving the peeled shrimp for another use.

Place the garlic, bay leaves and peppercorns into the center of a square of cheesecloth. Gather the edges of the cheesecloth together to form a bundle, and then tie it closed with kitchen string.

Add the cheesecloth bundle to the pot with the shrimp heads and shells, and then add the water. Bring to a boil over high heat, and then cover the pot and simmer over low heat for 30 minutes. Skim off and discard any foam that rises to the top with a spoon or ladle.

Remove and discard the cheesecloth bundle from the pot. Working in batches, blend the shrimp heads and shells, along with the liquid from the pot, in a blender. Blend until the shrimp heads and shells are completely puréed, making sure you use all the liquid from the pot.

Pour the stock through a fine mesh strainer and into a large bowl. Push on the solids in the strainer to extract as much liquid as possible. Discard the remaining solids in the strainer.

Allow the stock to cool completely before storing in the refrigerator for 2–3 days, or in the freezer for up to a month.

> **COOK'S NOTE:** You can substitute the shrimp shells and heads with 1 lb (500 g) of crab or lobster shells, or even fish heads and bones, to instead make a seafood stock. Just simmer the shells or bones with water as directed above, and then strain the stock after 30 minutes.
>
> Do not attempt to blend crab or lobster shells, or fish heads or bones, in your blender.

CHICKEN STOCK

Believe it or not, I find solace in making chicken stock. It's true. Maybe it's from the aroma of chicken soup that fills the house, or perhaps it's in knowing that the flavorful stock will be used to enrich so many other recipes down the road. Whatever it is, making chicken stock is one of my favorite things to do in the kitchen. I tend to stockpile a variety of raw chicken parts in my freezer for use in chicken stock—these parts are usually the backs and necks left from whole chickens I've previously processed. But if you are not of the chicken-bone-stashing ilk, I've found that more and more grocery stores are beginning to sell chicken backs, necks, and feet for those of us who love to make chicken stock on a whim. And if your store doesn't sell these parts separately, you can always purchase chicken wings on the cheap whenever you'd like to make stock.

Makes about 8 cups (about 1.75 liters)
Prep Time: 10 minutes
Cooking Time: 4 hours

2 lbs (1 kg) chicken bones and parts, such as wings, backs, feet, necks, etc.
2 bay leaves
1 teaspoon whole black peppercorns
1 stalk lemongrass, bottom 4–6 in (10–15 cm) trimmed and halved lengthwise
One 2-in (5-cm) piece fresh ginger, peeled and smashed with the side of a knife
8 cups (1.75 liters) water, plus more to cover as needed

Place the chicken bones in a large deep pot or Dutch oven. Pour in enough cold water to cover the bones by at least 1 in (2.5 cm), and then bring to a boil over high heat. Boil the chicken bones for 5 minutes, and then remove from the heat and pour the bones and water through a large colander set inside a sink. Rinse off the bones with cold running water, and rinse the pot out as well to remove any residue that may have been left behind. This first step helps to ensure a clear stock by removing any impurities from the chicken bones.

Return the chicken bones to the pot, along with the bay leaves, black peppercorns, lemongrass and ginger. Pour in the water— enough to cover the bones by at least 1 in (2.5 cm). Bring the pot to a boil, and then cover and gently simmer over low heat for at least 4 hours, occasionally skimming and discarding any foam or fat that rises to the surface of the liquid.

Pour the contents of the pot through a fine-mesh sieve set over a large bowl. Discard the solids in the sieve. Allow the stock to cool, and then store in containers in the refrigerator for up to 3 days, or freeze for up to 3 months.

> **COOK'S NOTE:** This stock can be used in multiple recipes throughout this cookbook, such as Chicken and Rice Porridge (page 54), Filipino Chicken Noodle Soup (page 67), Shrimp and Pork with Homemade Pancit Noodles (page 58), and Stir-Fried Wheat Flour Noodles with Shrimp and Vegetables (page 61).

PICKLED GREEN PAPAYA ATCHARA

Atchara (also *acharra*, or *atsara*) is a pickled Filipino dish usually comprised of shredded green papaya and carrots, and served as a condiment. It's similar in flavor to the pickled ginger served at sushi joints. As such, I think *atchara* makes for a great palate cleanser between bites and goes especially well with grilled meats. It's even great on top of grilled burgers as a type of pickled slaw.

Makes about 1 quart (1 liter)
Prep Time: 20 minutes
Cooking Time: 10 minutes, plus time to cool

2 cups (500 ml) white Filipino cane vinegar, or white distilled vinegar
½ cup (90 g) brown sugar
1 tablespoon salt
½ teaspoon freshly ground black pepper
One 1-in (2.5-cm) piece fresh ginger, peeled and cut into thin matchsticks
4 cloves garlic, minced
4 cups grated green papaya, about ¾ lb (350 g)
1 cup grated carrots, about ¼ lb (100 g)
1 small red onion, thinly sliced
1 teaspoon dried red pepper flakes

Combine the vinegar, sugar, salt, black pepper, ginger, and garlic in a medium saucepan over high heat. Bring to a boil and stir until the sugar and salt have dissolved. Remove from the heat and allow to cool slightly.

Meanwhile, combine the papaya, carrot, onion, and red pepper flakes in a large bowl. Pour the warm pickling liquid over the vegetables and toss to combine.

Allow the mixture to come to room temperature, and then place in an airtight container and refrigerate for at least 1 day before serving. The *atchara* will keep for up to 1 month in the refrigerator.

PINEAPPLE SWEET AND SOUR SAUCE

This is one of my favorite condiments to prepare because it goes well with just about everything. In addition to the obvious pairing with fried *lumpia*, I also use this dipping sauce for fried chicken, grilled fish, French fries, and even eggs. With sweetness from pineapple juice, tartness from vinegar, spice from ginger and a little heat from dried red pepper flakes, you too will find yourself often reaching for this sauce.

Makes about 1 cup (250 ml)
Prep Time: 5 minutes
Cooking Time: 10 minutes

2 teaspoons cornstarch
2 tablespoons water
¾ cup (185 ml) fresh or canned pineapple juice
2 tablespoons white Filipino cane vinegar, or cider vinegar
1 tablespoon soy sauce
One ½-in (1.25-cm) piece fresh ginger, peeled and minced
1 clove garlic, minced
2 teaspoons brown sugar
½ teaspoon dried red pepper flakes (optional)

Stir the cornstarch into the water and set aside. Combine the rest of the ingredients in a small saucepan over moderately high heat and bring to a boil, stirring to dissolve the sugar. Stir the cornstarch slurry into the saucepan, decrease the heat to low and simmer until the sauce thickens, 3–5 minutes.

Remove the sauce from the heat and allow to cool to room temperature before serving. The sauce will continue to thicken a bit more as it cools.

Serve as a sauce for Mini Spring Rolls with Pork and Shrimp (page 32), Crunchy Crab Lumpia (page 37), Pork and Vegetable Lumpia (page 30), Filipino-Style Fried Chicken (page 98), or Filipino Scotch Eggs (page 111).

TOMATO RELISH WITH FISH SAUCE AND SHALLOTS

KAMATIS, BAGOONG AT LASONA

Sweet, tangy, and savory, with a mild onion bite, this simple relish of chopped tomatoes and shallots dressed in fish sauce is the most commonly found condiment on my family's dinner table. This condiment is so common in the Northern Philippines that it is usually referred to by its Ilocano initials of "KBL" (*Kamatis, Bagoong, Lasona*/Tomatoes, Fish Sauce, Shallots). Although the term "*bagoong*" usually only refers to fermented shrimp or fish paste, fish sauce is often used in KBL depending on the preference of the household. Any ripe chopped tomato works well in this recipe, but I love the look of cherry tomatoes cut into quarters.

Makes about 2 cups (500 ml)
Prep Time: 5 minutes

½ lb (250 g) cherry tomatoes, quartered
2 tablespoons minced shallot
1–2 tablespoons fish sauce

Combine all the ingredients in a large bowl and toss gently to combine. Serve KBL alongside Crunchy Pork Belly (page 89), grilled meats and fish, or over steamed white rice.

VARIATIONS: Substitute 1 tablespoon of fresh minced ginger for 1 tablespoon of the minced shallot.

Substitute minced red onion, or sliced green onion (scallion), for the shallot.

FLAKY PASTRY PIE CRUST

This is a simple and basic pastry crust that can be used in multiple recipes throughout this cookbook. You can prepare this dough up to a day in advance before rolling it out for use in other recipes in this book such as Bitter Melon and Bacon Quiche (page 44), Chicken Adobo Pot Pies (page 74), Egg and Vegetable Turnovers (page 34), and Mini Mango Turnovers (page 122). Alternatively, you can substitute store-bought pie crust or puff pastry for this recipe.

Yields one 9-in (23-cm) pie crust
Prep Time: 10 minutes, plus at least 30 minutes rest in the refrigerator

1¼ cups (175 g) all-purpose flour
⅛ teaspoon salt
8 tablespoons cold butter, cut into small cubes
1 tablespoon cider vinegar
¼ cup (60 ml) ice water

In a large bowl, combine the flour and the salt. Using a pastry cutter, or your fingers, mix the butter into the flour until the mixture resembles pea-sized crumbs.

Add the vinegar and mix with your hands, or a rubber spatula, to incorporate. Add the water 1 tablespoon at a time, mixing until the dough just comes together to form a large ball and can hold its shape. You may not need to use all the water.

Alternatively, you can pulse the flour, salt and butter in a food processor until the mixture resembles pea-sized crumbs. Drizzle in the vinegar and pulse to combine, and then drizzle in the water, little by little, pulsing the food processor until the dough just comes together.

After the dough can hold its shape, form it into a thick disk and cover with plastic wrap. Place the dough in the refrigerator and let it rest for at least 30 minutes before rolling out.

HOMEMADE BANANA KETCHUP

Makes about 1½ cups (375 ml)
Prep Time: 10 minutes
Cooking Time: 45 minutes

A tomato shortage during World War II did not bode well for the Filipino's love of American ketchup. Luckily, Filipino food technologist, Maria Y. Orosa, created a sweet facsimile of ketchup using the plentiful local bananas grown all over the Islands. Though naturally a brownish-blonde hue, the newly created banana ketchup was dyed a bright red to resemble the old standard. Filipinos quickly embraced the fruitier condiment and soon, banana ketchup became just as popular in the Philippines as tomato ketchup was in the United States.

Though banana ketchup (or banana sauce) can be easily found at Asian markets, you can just as easily make your own banana ketchup at home—without all the artificial colors and flavors.

The color in my homemade ketchup comes from Annatto Oil (page 26) and tomato paste, so the finished product is a subtle orange hue rather than the familiar crimson red of store-bought ketchup. Despite this difference in color, the tangy-sweet flavor of this homemade ketchup is worlds better than the bottled artificial stuff at the Asian market.

Use this ketchup as you would any store-bought ketchup (tomato or banana), but it's especially good as a dip for Oven-Baked Sweet Potato Fries (page 38), atop Grilled Turkey Burgers (page 100), mixed into Filipino Spaghetti (page 64), or as a glaze for Filipino Meatloaf (page 83) and Grilled Lemongrass Chicken (page 84).

2 tablespoons Annatto Oil (page 26), or regular vegetable oil
1 small onion, chopped
2 cloves garlic, minced
1 tablespoon tomato paste
2 large ripe bananas, about ¾ lb (350 g) total, mashed
½ cup (125 ml) cider vinegar
¼ cup (65 ml) water
2 tablespoons brown sugar, plus more, to taste
½ teaspoon freshly ground black pepper
⅛ teaspoon ground clove
Pinch of salt
1 teaspoon soy sauce
1 bay leaf

Heat the oil in a medium saucepan over medium heat. Add the onion and cook until soft and translucent, 5–7 minutes. Add the garlic and tomato paste and stir to combine, cooking for 2–3 minutes until the tomato paste breaks down and melts into the onion and garlic.

Place the mashed banana into the pan and stir until they pick up a reddish-orange hue from the Annatto Oil (if using) and tomato paste. Pour in the vinegar and water, stirring to scrape up any browned bits from the bottom of the pan.

Add the brown sugar, black pepper, ground clove, salt, and soy sauce, and stir to combine. Drop the bay leaf into the pan and bring the mixture to a boil. Reduce heat to low and then simmer, partially covered, for 20–30 minutes. Remove from heat and discard the bay leaf.

Place the banana mixture into the carafe of a blender and purée until smooth. If the banana ketchup is too thick, it can be thinned out with additional water. Taste the ketchup for seasoning, and add more sugar if a sweeter ketchup is desired.

Store the banana ketchup in an airtight container in the refrigerator for 2–3 weeks.

COOK'S NOTE: For a spicier version of this ketchup, add 1–2 chopped Thai chili peppers (or 1 small jalapeño chili pepper) and sauté along with the onion and garlic. Continue with the rest of the recipe as written.

HOMEMADE MAYONNAISE

Because store-bought mayo is often so inexpensive and widely available, preparing this recipe is something rarely considered by the home cook. It is often dismissed as a task not worth the bother. So why make your own mayonnaise?

Because this Homemade Mayonnaise tastes so much better than store-bought, and it's surprisingly easy to make—that's why. And once you've got that jar of Annatto Oil (page 26) staring back at you, you're probably going to wonder how else you can use the amber oil. Well, when emulsified with an egg yolk, some salt, Filipino vinegar and citrus juice, that Annatto Oil can easily transform into the best, and most vibrantly colorful mayonnaise you've ever had.

You can simply use a whisk to bring the mayonnaise together, but an electric hand mixer makes for quicker work—and is easier on your whisking arm.

Makes about 1 cup (250 ml)
Prep Time: 10 minutes

1 large egg yolk
½ teaspoon salt
1 teaspoon Filipino coconut vinegar, or white distilled vinegar
2 teaspoons fresh *calamansi* juice, or fresh lemon juice
¾ cup (185 ml) Annatto Oil (page 26), or regular vegetable oil

Combine the yolk, salt, vinegar, and *calamansi* juice in a large bowl, and whisk until light and frothy. While whisking constantly, drizzle in a few drops of the oil to begin an emulsification. Drizzle in a few more drops of oil and continue to whisk vigorously until the mixture thickens a bit, 2–3 minutes.

Gradually add the remaining oil in a slow, thin stream, whisking constantly, until the mixture thickens and a mayonnaise is formed, about 3–5 minutes more. Cover the mayonnaise and store in the refrigerator for up to a week.

You can use this Homemade Mayonnaise as you would any other mayonnaise, and you can also use it in the Crunchy Crab Lumpia recipe (page 37), as well as in the Grilled Turkey Burger recipe (page 100).

> **COOK'S NOTES:** To prevent your bowl from moving as you whisk, place a moist paper towel underneath the bowl.
> To make an *aioli*, whisk in 1 minced garlic clove before adding the oil.
> For a spicy mayonnaise, whisk in a few squirts of Sriracha hot sauce after the mayonnaise has formed.

ANNATTO OIL ACHUETE

With its subtle flavor and brilliant color, Annatto Oil is often used to lend a familiar orange hue to many Filipino dishes such as Braised Oxtail with Roasted Vegetables in Peanut Sauce (page 86), Shrimp and Pork with Homemade Pancit Noodles (page 58), and Grilled Lemongrass Chicken (page 84), just to name a few. But don't limit its use to just Filipino recipes—use it as you would any other cooking oil. Annatto seeds can be found in Asian and Latin markets, and from online retailers.

Makes about 2 cups (500 ml)
Prep Time: 5 minutes
***Cooking Time: 10 minutes,
    plus 1–2 hours to steep***

2 cups (500 ml) canola oil
½ cup (100 g) annatto seeds
2 teaspoons whole black
    peppercorns
1 bay leaf

Combine all of the ingredients in a large saucepan over moderately high heat. Warm the oil until it just begins to bubble. Remove from heat and set aside to steep for 1–2 hours.

Strain the oil through a fine mesh strainer, discarding the solids in the strainer. Store the Annatto Oil in an airtight container for 3–4 weeks in the refrigerator.

SAUTÉED SHRIMP PASTE GINISANG BAGOONG

Fermented shrimp paste (*bagoong*) is made from tiny shrimp preserved in salt. On its own, *bagoong* is a very pungent condiment primarily used to add a savory and salty kick to many Filipino dishes. But, when sautéed with shallot and garlic, the harshness of the shrimp paste is softened a bit. Don't get me wrong, the sautéed version is still plenty pungent and salty, but in a less bracing way, because it is cut with the sweetness of the shallot, garlic, and a bit of sugar. Fermented shrimp paste can be found in Asian markets labeled as "*Bagoong Alamang.*" I prefer *bagoong* that isn't dyed bright pink, but the pink variety is fine to use too.

Makes ½ cup (250 g)
Prep Time: 5 minutes
Cooking Time: 10 minutes

1 tablespoon high-heat
    cooking oil
1 tablespoon minced shallot
1 tablespoon minced garlic
1–2 Thai chili peppers, thinly
    sliced (optional)
½ cup (250 g) fermented shrimp
    paste (*Bagoong Alamang*)
2 teaspoons sugar
½ teaspoon freshly ground
    black pepper

Heat a large wok or sauté pan over high heat until a drop of water sizzles and evaporates on contact. Swirl in the oil and add the shallot, stir-frying until the shallot wilts and begins to lightly brown, 2–3 minutes. Add the garlic and chili peppers (if using) and cook until the garlic just begins to brown, 1–2 minutes.

Stir in the shrimp paste, sugar and black pepper and toss and cook for 3–5 minutes more.

> **COOK'S NOTES:** Serve *Ginisang Bagoong* with Braised Oxtail with Roasted Vegetables and Peanut Sauce (page 86). Just dab some of the sautéed shrimp paste onto each spoonful of stew and rice.
>
> For a salty-sour Filipino snack, dip slices of fresh green mango into the sautéed shrimp paste.

GARLIC VINEGAR DIPPING SAUCE

I like to call this condiment "house *lumpia* sauce" as it is often used as a dipping sauce for fried *lumpia* in many Filipino households—though it is versatile enough to be used for more than just *lumpia*. With a vinegar tang and garlicky bite, this sauce is perfect for cutting through the richness of many fried and grilled foods.

You can choose any Filipino vinegar (page 19) for use in this sauce, as well as cider, rice wine, or white distilled vinegars.

Makes ½ cup (125 ml)
Prep Time: 5 minutes

½ cup (125 ml) vinegar
1 tablespoon minced garlic
1 teaspoon freshly ground black pepper
¼ teaspoon dried red pepper flakes (optional)
Heavy pinch of salt

Whisk together all of the ingredients in a small bowl. Serve as a dipping sauce for spring rolls, *empanadas*, or grilled meats.

SOY AND CITRUS DIPPING SAUCE
TOYOMANSI

A mixture of soy sauce and citrus juice may sound simple enough, but these two ingredients enliven everything from grilled fish to noodles.

I like to use a 1 to 1 ratio of soy and citrus, but you can adjust the salty-sour balance to suit your own taste.

Makes ½ cup (125 ml)
Prep Time: 5 minutes

¼ cup (65 ml) soy sauce
¼ cup (65 ml) fresh *calamansi* juice, or fresh lemon juice

Whisk together the soy sauce and citrus juice in a small bowl. Serve with grilled fish, *pancit* noodles, or fried foods.

SPICY LIME AND FISH SAUCE DIP

Similar to Soy and Citrus Dipping Sauce (below left), this sauce strikes a balance between salty and sour, but with a bit more depth of flavor from the fish sauce and the sliced chilies. Try it with seafood dishes.

Makes ½ cup (125 ml)
Prep Time: 5 minutes

¼ cup (65 ml) fish sauce
¼ cup (65 ml) fresh *calamansi* juice, or fresh lime juice
2–3 Thai chili peppers, stemmed and thinly sliced

Whisk together all of the ingredients in a small bowl. Serve with grilled or fried fish and shellfish.

Spicy Lime and Fish Sauce Dip

Garlic Vinegar Dipping Sauce

Soy and Citrus Dipping Sauce

CHAPTER 1

APPETIZERS
PAMPAGANA

The appetizers in Filipino cuisine are usually served "family-style" together with the rest of the meal, rather than as a separate course as is commonly done in the West. Either way, the small bites and finger foods in this section—from crisp *lumpia* spring rolls to raw Filipino *ceviche*—will get you and your dinner guests primed for the rest of the meal to come. This is fitting considering that the Filipino term for appetizers, *pampagana*, translates to "whet the appetite."

PORK AND VEGETABLE LUMPIA

When I was in college, two things—and two things alone—encouraged my two-hour drive back to my parents' house at least once a month: laundry and *lumpia*.

The need for clean laundry goes without saying, but no trip home would be complete without a fresh supply of my mother's spring rolls filled with seasoned pork and vegetables. My mother would often make dozens of *lumpia* in one sitting. But instead of frying her bounty right away, she would place her freshly made *lumpia* in freezer bags that I would eagerly take back to my cramped apartment. My mother's *lumpia* could last forever in the freezer, but since they were so easy for me to prepare (I'd just take them out of the freezer, put them in hot oil, and fry until golden and crisp), my stash only seemed to last a few weeks. Oddly enough, my supply of *lumpia* almost always correlated with my supply of clean clothes. But after all, it'd be silly to go home just for laundry, wouldn't it?

Today, I've got my own washer and dryer and I've since learned to make my mother's *lumpia*. Strangely enough, though, I still find other reasons to visit my parents on the weekends.

Makes about 2 dozen spring rolls
Prep Time: 45 minutes
Cooking Time: 10 minutes

For the filling:
2 tablespoons high-heat cooking oil, plus more
   for frying
1 small onion, diced
4 cloves garlic, minced
1 lb (500 g) ground pork
1 tablespoon fish sauce
½ teaspoon freshly ground black pepper
1 cup (70 g) grated carrot
1 cup (70 g) mung bean sprouts
½ cup (65 g) frozen peas
25 square spring roll wrappers (8 x 8 in/20 x 20 cm),
   thawed
Water, for sealing the spring rolls

Heat a large wok or sauté pan over high heat until a drop of water sizzles and evaporates on contact. Swirl the oil into the pan and then add the onion and stir-fry until the onion wilts and begins to lightly brown, 2–3 minutes. Add the garlic and cook until the garlic just begins to brown, 1–2 minutes. Stir in the ground pork and cook for 1 minute, using a spatula or wooden spoon to break the meat into small pieces. Add the fish sauce, black pepper, carrot, bean sprouts and peas and stir to combine. Continue cooking until the meat is cooked through and the vegetables are tender, 3–4 minutes.

Transfer the cooked filling to a fine-mesh sieve set over a large bowl and set aside. Draining the filling helps to prevent soggy spring rolls, allow the filling to drain and cool completely. After the filling has cooled, discard any liquid that has accumulated in the bowl and then transfer the filling into the same bowl.

Follow the illustrated instructions to the right for more information on how to fill and roll the *lumpia*.

To fry the *lumpia*, fill a large frying pan with at least a ½ in (1.25 cm) of vegetable oil. Heat over moderately high heat until the oil reaches 350°F (175°C) on a deep fry thermometer. Alternatively, you can drop a small piece of *lumpia* wrapper into the hot oil; if it sizzles and immediately begins to brown, the oil is hot enough and ready for frying.

When the oil is ready, fry the *lumpia* in batches, being careful to not overcrowd the pan. Fry the *lumpia*, turning occasionally, until golden and crisp, 3–4 minutes total. If frying frozen *lumpia*, add 1 minute of cook time to each side. Transfer the fried *lumpia* to a paper towel-lined plate to drain.

Serve with Garlic Vinegar Dipping Sauce (page 27) or Pineapple Sweet and Sour Sauce (page 22).

HOW TO ROLL THE LUMPIA

1. To roll the *lumpia*, place 1 spring roll wrapper on a clean, dry work surface so that one corner of the wrapper is pointing at you (positioned like a diamond, rather than a square). Place 1 heaping tablespoon of the filling just under the midpoint of the diamond, closest to the corner pointing at you.

2. Take the corner closest to you and roll it up and over the filling, until half of the wrapper remains.

3. Fold the left and right corners of the wrapper over the filling.

4. Using your fingers, or a pastry brush, dab the edges of the wrapper with water, and then continue to roll the *lumpia* toward the final corner at the top.

Place the finished *lumpia* aside, underneath a moist towel, and continue rolling until all of the filling has been used.

To freeze the *lumpia*, place them in a single layer on a baking sheet and place in the freezer until completely frozen. Transfer the frozen *lumpia* to a large resealable food storage bag and store in the freezer for up to 3 months.

MINI SPRING ROLLS WITH PORK AND SHRIMP
LUMPIA SHANGHAI

Although all *lumpia* are of Chinese origin, Lumpia Shanghai seems to scream its connection to China by name alone. Though Lumpia Shanghai really have nothing to do with the city of Shanghai itself, the spring roll's filling of ground pork, and its pairing with a sweet and sour dipping sauce (rather than a garlic and vinegar dipping sauce), are obvious tells of its Chinese roots.

Lumpia Shanghai are also usually thinner and smaller than their other fried counterparts. And because no fancy folding of the *lumpia* wrapper is required, Lumpia Shanghai are also relatively easy to prepare.

For a contrast in flavor and texture, my Lumpia Shanghai are filled with ground pork and minced shrimp, and they also have a spicy ginger kick as well. These Lumpia Shanghai are fantastic alone, or when served with Pineapple Sweet and Sour Sauce (page 22).

Makes 40–50 mini spring rolls
Prep Time: 30 minutes
Cooking Time: 10 minutes

For the wrappers:
25 square spring roll wrappers
  (8 x 8 in/20 x 20 cm), thawed
Water, for sealing *lumpia*
Oil, for frying

For the filling:
1 cup (70 g) grated carrot
One 2-in (5-cm) piece fresh ginger,
  peeled and minced
4 cloves garlic, minced
2 green onions (scallions), trimmed and
  thinly sliced (white and green parts)
½ lb (250 g) peeled and deveined raw
  shrimp, minced
1 lb (500 g) ground pork
1 tablespoon soy sauce
1 tablespoon oyster sauce
1 teaspoon freshly ground black pepper
1 egg, beaten

HOW TO ROLL THE LUMPIA SHANGHAI

1. Using a serrated knife, cut the square *lumpia* wrappers in half so that you have two stacks of rectangular wrappers. Place a damp paper towel over the wrappers to keep them from drying out as you work.

2. Place one of the rectangular wrappers vertically on your work surface with the short edge facing you. Place just a heaping teaspoon of the filling on the wrapper about a ½ in (1.25 cm) from the edge closest to you.

3. Grasp the bottom edge of the wrapper and roll it up and over the filling, continuing to roll until 2 in (5 cm) of wrapper remain.

4. Dip two fingers into a bowl of water, and then moisten the last 2 in (5 cm) of the wrapper with your fingers. Finish rolling the *lumpia*, and then rest it on its seam.

Place all of the ingredients for the filling in a large bowl and gently mix until thoroughly combined.

To roll the *lumpia*, follow the illustrated steps on the facing page.

To fry the *lumpia*, fill a large frying pan with about ½ in (1.25 cm) of oil. Heat the oil over moderately high heat until the oil reaches 350°F (175°C) on a deep fry thermometer. Alternatively, you can also drop a small piece of *lumpia* wrapper into the oil, if it begins to immediately brown and sizzle, the oil is ready.

Gently place the *lumpia* into the hot oil and fry until golden brown on all sides, 3 to 5 minutes total (if frying frozen *lumpia*, add 1 to 2 minutes cook time to each side).

Drain the fried *lumpia* on a plate lined with paper towels and serve immediately.

COOK'S NOTES: Re-freeze any unused *lumpia* wrappers.
To freeze the *lumpia*, place them on a baking sheet and place in the freezer until completely frozen. Transfer the frozen *lumpia* to a large, resealable food storage bag and store in the freezer for up to 3 months.

EGG AND VEGETABLE TURNOVERS
EMPANADAS

A holdover from Spanish colonialism, the *empanada* has become a favorite snack across the Philippines. Depending on the region, *empanadas* can be baked or deep-fried and are filled with everything from pork, sweet potatoes and raisins, to sour sausage and green papaya. In fact, my favorite incarnation of *empanadas* hail from the city of Batac in the Northern Philippines. The Batac *empanada* is a crispy, deep-fried parcel stuffed with shredded green papaya, mung bean sprouts, local sausage, and a whole egg. If that sounds like a lot of filling for a small *empanada*, it is. But Batac *empanadas* are nearly the size of a dinner plate! My version of Batac *empanadas* are baked, rather than fried, and they are a bit daintier in size as well. In addition to mung bean sprouts and shredded green papaya laced with sharp vinegar, a whole quail egg is cracked into the center of these *empanadas*, creating a rich flavorful filling for the flaky crust. Fresh quail eggs can be found at Asian markets, but they can be omitted from the recipe entirely.

Makes 12 empanadas
Prep Time: 30 minutes
Cooking Time: 30 minutes

HOW TO ROLL THE EMPANADA DOUGH

1. Remove the prepared Flaky Pastry Pie Crust dough (page 23) from the refrigerator and place on a clean, lightly floured work surface.

2. Form the dough into a cylinder shape, and then gently press and roll the dough with your palms to stretch it into a 12-in (30-cm) long log. Using a knife, divide the log into two 6-in (15-cm) pieces.

3. Cut each log into 6 equal pieces to yield 12 pieces of dough total. Using a rolling pin, roll each of the dough pieces until they are roughly ⅛-in (3-mm) thick by 5 in (13 cm) in diameter.

4. Dust the dough with flour as necessary to keep it from sticking. Place the discs of *empanada* dough on a parchment lined baking sheet and in the refrigerator until ready to fill.

For the filling:
1 tablespoon high-heat cooking oil
1 cup (100 g) chopped onion
4 cloves garlic, minced
1–2 Thai chili peppers, thinly sliced (optional)
1 cup (70 g) mung bean sprouts
1 cup (70 g) grated green papaya
1 tablespoon dark Filipino cane vinegar (*sukang Iloco*),
   or apple cider vinegar
1 teaspoon coarse salt
½ teaspoon freshly ground black pepper
12 fresh quail eggs (optional)

For the crust:
1 recipe Flaky Pastry Pie Crust (page 23), or
   store-bought pie crust
1 large egg, beaten

Preheat the oven to 375°F (190°C).

To make the filling, heat a large wok or sauté pan over high heat until a drop of water sizzles and evaporates on contact. Swirl the oil into the pan, and then add the onion and stir-fry until the onion wilts and begins to lightly brown, 2–3 minutes. Add the garlic and chili peppers (if using) and cook until the garlic just begins to brown, 30 seconds to 1 minute.

Stir in the bean sprouts, green papaya, vinegar, salt, and pepper and toss to combine. Continue cooking until the papaya cooks down and wilts, and the pan is nearly dry, 2–3 minutes. Remove from the heat and allow the mixture to cool completely.

Meanwhile, if using Flaky Pastry Pie Crust (page 23) roll out the dough for the *empanadas* as shown on the facing page. If using store-bought pie crust, cut out 12 rounds of dough that are each 4–5 in (10–13 cm) in diameter.

To fill the *empanadas*, place a tablespoon of the cooled filling in the center of each disc of prepared dough. If using quail eggs, form a well in the center of the vegetable filling and carefully crack a quail egg into each well. Gently fold the circle of dough over the filling to form a half moon. Carefully press the edges of the dough around the filling to get rid of any air pockets, and then gently crimp and seal the edges of the dough with the tines of a fork. Brush the top surface of the *empanadas* with the beaten egg, and then place on a baking sheet lined with parchment paper.

Bake the *empanadas* in the oven until the crust is golden brown, 25–30 minutes. Serve the *empanadas* with Garlic Vinegar Dipping Sauce (page 27).

COOK'S NOTE: You can also add a small amount of cooked *longganisa* sausage to the filling as well. Just reduce the amount of bean sprouts and green papaya by half. Then cook 2–3 patties of *longganisa* (page 93) in a separate pan from the vegetable filling, breaking the patties up with a wooden spoon or spatula as you cook them. Then add 1–2 teaspoons of the cooked meat to the *empanadas*.

GARLICKY POPCORN

Tinged with a faint orange hue from the Annatto Oil and paprika, this garlicky and smoky homemade popcorn makes for a great appetizer when entertaining guests, or as a quick TV snack when sitting on the couch with a loved one. You won't touch the microwaved stuff after tasting this popcorn.

Serves 2–4 as a snack
Prep Time: 5 minutes
Cooking Time: 5 minutes

½ teaspoon salt
½ teaspoon garlic powder
½ teaspoon smoked Spanish
   paprika, or regular paprika
3 tablespoons Annatto Oil
   (page 26), or regular
   vegetable oil
½ cup (100 g) popcorn
   kernels
3 tablespoons butter

Combine the salt, garlic powder and paprika in a small bowl and mix until thoroughly combined. Set the spice mixture aside.

Heat the oil in a large pot over moderately high heat for 1–2 minutes. Place 4–5 popcorn kernels into the pot and cover the pot. As soon as you hear the kernels pop, place the rest of the kernels into the pot, cover, and gently shake the pot back and forth over the burner. The kernels will begin popping all at once.

Continue to gently move the pot back and forth over the burner until the popping subsides, 2–3 minutes more. When you can no longer hear any kernels popping, remove the pot from the heat.

Transfer the popcorn from the pot and into a large bowl. Add the butter to the pot—the pot will still be hot enough to melt the butter. Sprinkle the spice mix onto the popcorn and toss to thoroughly combine. Drizzle the melted butter over the popcorn. Serve immediately.

FILIPINO MACKEREL "CEVICHE" KINILAW NA TANGUIGUE

Serves 4
Prep Time: 15 minutes
Cooking Time: 10 minutes

Kinilaw is a method of food preparation that usually features raw seafood quickly bathed in vinegar, citrus juice, or a combination of both. Although seafood is the most common type of *kinilaw*, raw vegetables, and even raw meat, can also be prepared in this fashion.

While *kinilaw* is indigenous to the Philippines, it is similar to Latin American *ceviche* in that the seafood can be dressed in citrus juice. However, the similarities end there. Where the raw fish in a *ceviche* is drastically transformed and "cooked" after a lengthy marination time, the raw fish in a *kinilaw* retains its freshness after only a few brief moments in a sour bath. In fact, because the fish is still very much raw when served, *kinilaw* may be closer to a Japanese *sashimi* than a Latin American *ceviche*.

Fresh cucumbers and radish provide crunch and texture to this *kinilaw*, while vinegar, shallots, ginger, and chili peppers lend bright sharp flavors to highlight the raw fish. While mackerel is a very traditional choice for *kinilaw*, I also like using mackerel because it's an abundant and sustainable fish that is locally available to me. If you can't find mackerel, or if you just don't like the rich oily flavor of mackerel, any *sashimi*-grade fish (salmon, tuna, yellowtail, etc.) that is locally available to you can be used in this recipe.

¼ cup (10 g) unsweetened, dried shredded coconut
1 lb (500 g) fresh *sashimi*-grade, mackerel fillets (or other fresh *sashimi*-grade fish)
1 tablespoon minced shallot
One 1-in (2.5-cm) piece fresh ginger, peeled and minced
1 small cucumber, peeled, deseeded and diced
4 red radishes, trimmed, halved lengthwise and cut into thin half moons
1–2 Thai chili peppers, thinly sliced (optional)
¼ cup (65 ml) Filipino coconut vinegar, or unseasoned rice vinegar
1 teaspoon coarse salt
½ teaspoon freshly ground black pepper
Fresh *calamansi* limes, halved, or regular lime wedges, for spritzing

Preheat the oven to 325°F (160°C)

Spread the shredded coconut into an even layer on a baking sheet. Place the coconut in the oven and toast until golden brown, stirring once, 8–10 minutes. Remove the toasted coconut from the oven and allow to cool completely.

Using clean tweezers, remove any pin bones from the mackerel fillets. Cut the mackerel into ½-in (1.25-cm) cubes and then place into a large bowl. Cover the bowl with plastic wrap and place in the refrigerator until ready to serve.

Combine the shallot, ginger, cucumber, radishes, and Thai chili peppers (if using) in a medium bowl. Cover the bowl with plastic wrap and place in the refrigerator until ready to serve.

When ready to serve, add the contents from the medium bowl to the cubed fish in the large bowl. Add the vinegar, salt, and black pepper to the large bowl and toss gently until everything is combined and all of the fish has been dressed in the vinegar.

Portion the *kinilaw* into individual serving dishes and then garnish each serving with the toasted coconut. Serve immediately.

CRUNCHY CRAB LUMPIA

A few years ago, my wife and I vacationed at a beautiful beach resort on Boracay Island in the Philippines. Aside from the clear azure waters and pristine white sand beaches, one of my lasting memories from that trip was… a plate of chili crab. That's right. Chili crab. A simple Southeast Asian dish of fresh crabs cooked in a spicy chili sauce. The chili crab we had in Boracay was prepared from some very fresh, just-caught crabs that we purchased at the wet market one day. We then had our fresh catch prepared at a nearby restaurant just a few paces down from the wet market. Soon, our still-kicking-and-nipping crabs were transformed into a steaming plate of shellfish varnished with a fiery, lip-numbing glaze. It was a messy endeavor, cracking open those crabs, but I made sure to suck and slurp every last bit of meat and spicy sauce from the crab shells. I was so taken with that chili crab in Boracay, that I was inspired to make my own version at home—but in spring roll form. My spicy Crunchy Crab Lumpia is a great way to turn canned crab meat, or even imitation crab, into something that is delectably spicy. You can also very easily adjust the spiciness of these spring rolls by decreasing or omitting the chili peppers and chili paste. And finally, the only shells left to deal with are the crisp golden shells of the lumpia wrapper.

Makes about 2 dozen spring rolls
Prep Time: 45 minutes
Cooking Time: 10 minutes

1 tablespoon high-heat cooking oil, plus more for frying
1 tablespoon minced shallot
2 cloves garlic, minced
1–2 Thai chili peppers, stemmed and minced (optional)
8 oz (250 g) shredded Napa cabbage
½ teaspoon salt
1 lb (500 g) canned crab meat, or flaked imitation crab, drained
2 tablespoons Homemade Mayonnaise (page 25), or regular store-bought mayonnaise
2 tablespoons sambal oelek chili paste (optional)
4 tablespoons chopped fresh coriander leaves (cilantro)
½ teaspoon freshly ground black pepper
25 square spring roll wrappers (8 x 8 in/20 x 20 cm), thawed
Water, for sealing the spring rolls

Heat a large wok or sauté pan over high heat until a drop of water sizzles and evaporates on contact. Swirl the oil into the pan and add the shallot, garlic, and chili peppers (if using) and stir-fry until the garlic begins to lightly brown, about 30 seconds. Add the cabbage and salt to the pan and toss to combine, continuing to cook until the cabbage wilts down and softens, 2–3 minutes. Remove the pan from the heat and allow the cabbage mixture to cool completely.

Combine the cooled cabbage mixture with the crab meat, mayonnaise, chili paste (if using), coriander leaves, and black pepper in a large bowl. Gently mix the contents in the bowl until thoroughly combined.

Follow the illustrated instructions on page 31 for more information on how to fill and roll the lumpia.

To fry the lumpia, fill a large frying pan with at least ½ in (1.25 cm) of a high-heat cooking oil. Heat over moderately high heat until the oil reaches 350°F (175°C) on a deep fry thermometer. Alternatively, you can insert a dry wooden skewer or chopstick into the hot oil; if bubbles quickly rise to the surface around the stick, the oil is hot enough and ready for frying.

When the oil is ready, fry the lumpia in batches, being careful to not overcrowd the pan. Fry the lumpia, turning occasionally, until golden and crisp, 3–4 minutes total. If frying frozen lumpia, add 1 minute of cook time to each side. Transfer the fried lumpia to a paper towel-lined plate to drain.

Serve the Crunchy Crab Lumpia with Spicy Lime and Fish Sauce Dip (page 27), or with Pineapple Sweet and Sour Sauce (page 22).

Serves 4–6
Prep Time: 10 minutes
Cooking Time: 30 minutes

2 lbs (1 kg) sweet potatoes (about 2 large sweet potatoes)
2 tablespoons Annatto Oil (page 26), or regular vegetable oil
1 teaspoon sugar
1 teaspoon salt
½ teaspoon garlic powder
½ teaspoon freshly ground black pepper
¼ teaspoon smoked Spanish paprika, or regular paprika

Place 2 sheet pans lined with foil onto separate racks in the oven and preheat the oven to 450°F (230°C).

Peel the sweet potatoes and trim off the ends. Cut the sweet potatoes into planks or wedges that are a ¼-in (6-mm) wide by ¼-in (6-mm) thick. It's important to cut the potatoes as uniformly as possible so that they bake evenly.

Place the sweet potatoes into a large bowl, and then add the Annatto Oil. Toss well to coat.

Add the rest of the ingredients to a small bowl and stir well to combine. Sprinkle the spice mixture over the potatoes and toss to evenly coat.

Carefully remove the hot foil-lined sheet pans from the oven and spread the sweet potatoes out in a single layer onto each pan. Place the sweet potatoes in the oven and bake for 15 minutes. Rotate the sheet pans to ensure even cooking, and then continue to bake until the sweet potatoes are tender and the edges are brown and crisp, 10–15 minutes more.

Remove the potatoes from the oven and allow to cool slightly before serving. Serve with Homemade Banana Ketchup (page 24).

OVEN–BAKED SWEET POTATO FRIES KAMOTE FRIES

Because orange-fleshed sweet potatoes are used so frequently in Filipino cooking, sweet potato fries have become just as popular in the Philippines (where they are known as *kamote* fries) as they have at various bars and pubs here in the United States. Although my version of these fries is baked in the oven, they are just as delicious as their fried counterparts. A light spice coating of sugar, salt, garlic powder and paprika make these baked fries an addictively salty-sweet treat.

SHRIMP AND SWEET POTATO FRITTERS UKOY

Ukoy are deep-fried fritters that usually feature a web of shredded vegetables (such as sweet potatoes, green papaya, and mung bean sprouts) studded with tiny dried shrimp and bound together by a light rice flour batter. The crispy fritters are so popular in the Philippines that variations can be found everywhere from street vendors, to home kitchens, to upscale restaurants. When developing my own *ukoy* recipe for this book, I couldn't resist adding sweetened shredded coconut to my batter. The result is a sweet and savory play on coconut shrimp in the form of a crisp Filipino fritter.

Makes about 12 fritters
Prep Time: 20 minutes
Cooking Time: 15 minutes

½ cup (70 g) rice flour
2 tablespoons all-purpose flour
½ teaspoon salt
½ teaspoon freshly ground black pepper
1 large egg, beaten
½ cup (125 ml) beer, divided
½ lb (250 g) raw medium-sized shrimp, peeled and deveined
1 cup (125 g) peeled and grated sweet potato
1 cup (75 g) sweetened shredded coconut
Oil, for frying

Combine the rice flour, all-purpose flour, salt and black pepper in a large bowl. Add the egg and ¼ cup (65 ml) of the beer and whisk well to combine. Slowly whisk in the rest of the beer, little by little, until the mixture resembles pancake batter—slightly thick, but still loose and runny. You may not have to use all of the beer.

Roughly chop the raw shrimp into ½-in (1.25-cm) chunks, and then add the chopped shrimp to the batter. Add the sweet potato and coconut and stir until everything is well combined and the batter is evenly distributed. Place the batter in the refrigerator for at least 10 minutes—this allows the batter to firm up so it won't break apart while frying.

Pour enough oil into a large heavy skillet so that it reaches a depth of 1 in (2.5 cm). Heat the oil over moderately high heat until the oil reaches 350°F (175°C) on a deep fry thermometer. Alternatively, you can also drop a battered piece of sweet potato or coconut into the oil—if the batter immediately begins to sizzle and brown, the oil is hot enough and ready for frying.

When the oil is hot, form the fritters by carefully dropping a heaping tablespoon of the batter into the hot oil, and then gently pressing on the fritter to slightly flatten it. Fry 3–4 fritters at a time, being careful to not overcrowd the pan. Fry the fritters, turning once, until golden brown on both sides—3–4 minutes total. Drain the fritters on a large plate lined with paper towels.

Serve the fritters immediately, with a dipping sauce of Homemade Banana Ketchup (page 24), or Garlic Vinegar Dipping Sauce (page 27), or Pineapple Sweet and Sour Sauce (page 22).

CHAPTER 2

VEGETABLES AND SALADS
GULAY AT ENSALADA

Yes, with such famously porky dishes as *lechon* (roast pig), *lechon kawali* (Crunchy Pork Belly, page 89) and *sisig* (Spicy Sizzling Pork, page 112), Filipinos may have a reputation as having a deep penchant for all things pig. But don't let this reputation fool you. Because of the natural botanical bounty of the Philippines, there are a number of incredibly delicious vegetable dishes that can either serve as a light counterpoint to richer dishes (yes, like pork), or they can be served on their own with rice for a light lunch or dinner. I wanted to share and highlight a few of the fruits and vegetables commonly used in the Philippines, but can be easily found in Asian markets. So in this section, you'll find a light and refreshing salad that pairs sour green mangoes with crunchy *jicama* and soft vermicelli noodles, as well as a unique and flavorful *quiche* that showcases bitter melon with bacon. I also provide a family favorite recipe for *pinakbet* (Stewed Vegetables with Pork Belly, page 49)—a rustic stew that emphasizes an abundance of Filipino vegetables. In addition, I also provide a number of recipes using vegetables that can be more easily found at regular grocery stores. Quick, no-fuss stir-fries of mung bean sprouts or green beans are sure to please, as well as a rich dish of kale braised in coconut milk, or eggs baked with smoky eggplant and tomatoes. And if the vegetables in this section aren't enough, I also have a number of more substantial vegetable dishes in the Soups, Noodles, and Rice section (page 50), as well as in the Adobo section (page 68). Who says Filipinos don't eat vegetables?

BEAN SPROUTS WITH TOFU GINISANG TOGUE AT TOKWA

It's not often that I get excited over tofu, but when it's quickly stir-fried with crisp mung bean sprouts and glazed in a slightly sweet and spicy sauce, I'm all in. This quick Filipino stir-fry makes for a great light lunch, or as part of a multi-course meal. As with all stir-frys, it's important to have your ingredients prepped beforehand since this dish comes together and cooks so quickly. It's also important that the tofu be as dry as possible when stir-frying in order to achieve a beautiful brown crust with a silky interior.

Serves 4–6 as part of a multi-course meal
Prep Time: 15 minutes
Cooking Time: 10 minutes

2 tablespoons oil, divided
One 12-oz (350-g) package firm tofu, rinsed and drained
1 small red onion, thinly sliced
4 cloves garlic, minced
1 carrot, peeled and cut into thin matchsticks
12 oz (350 g) mung bean sprouts
2 tablespoons oyster sauce
1–2 teaspoons *sambal oelek* chili paste (optional)
½ teaspoon freshly ground black pepper
2 green onions (scallions), thinly sliced (white and green parts)

Cut the tofu into ½-in (1.25-cm) cubes. Pat the tofu dry with paper towels and set aside.

Heat a large wok or sauté pan over high heat until a drop of water sizzles and evaporates on contact. Swirl in 1 tablespoon of the oil and add the dried tofu in a single layer to the pan. Cook the tofu, undisturbed, until it is nicely seared and browned, 1–2 minutes. Toss and stir-fry the tofu for another minute until it begins to lightly brown on all the other sides. Transfer the tofu to a platter and set aside.

Swirl in the remaining 1 tablespoon of oil into the pan. Add the onion and stir-fry until the pieces wilt and begin to lightly brown, 2–3 minutes. Add the garlic and carrot, and cook until the garlic just begins to brown, 1–2 minutes.

Add the mung bean sprouts and toss everything to combine. Return the tofu to the pan, and then add the oyster sauce, chili paste (if using), and black pepper. Gently toss everything to combine, being careful not to break up the tofu. Continue stir-frying for 1–2 minutes more until the mung bean sprouts are heated through, but are still crunchy. Remove from the heat and garnish with the green onion. Serve immediately.

GREEN BEANS WITH SHALLOTS AND GARLIC GINISANG BAGUIO BEANS

Because of its cool rainy climate, the mountain city of Baguio is widely known as "The Summer Capital of the Philippines." But besides being a summer respite for tourists and travelers, Baguio also provides a cooler climate for growing crops not necessarily native to the islands—crops like strawberries and green beans.

In fact, green beans in the Philippines are often called "Baguio Beans" to differentiate the verdant pods from the more common long beans (page 16) that are frequently used in Filipino dishes. Baguio beans are best when cooked simply—a quick stir-fry in oyster sauce, shallots, and garlic makes for a simple, yet delicious, side dish.

Serves 4–6
Prep Time: 5 minutes
Cooking Time: 10 minutes

1 teaspoon salt
1 lb (500 g) green beans, trimmed
1 tablespoon oil
2 tablespoons minced shallot
1 tablespoon minced garlic
1 tablespoon oyster sauce
½ teaspoon freshly ground black pepper

Bring 6 cups (1.5 liters) of water to a boil in a large saucepan over high heat. Add the salt and the green beans and cook for 3 minutes. Drain the beans and set aside.

Heat a large wok or sauté pan over high heat until a drop of water sizzles and evaporates on contact. Swirl the oil into the pan, and then add the shallot and garlic, and stir-fry until the garlic begins to lightly brown, 30 seconds to 1 minute. Add the beans and oyster sauce, and toss to combine, cooking until the beans are tender but still *al dente*, 3–4 minutes.

Season with the black pepper and serve immediately.

BITTER MELON AND BACON QUICHE

My parents and grandparents all hail from the Ilocos region of the Northern Philippines—a region known for its soulful home cooked meals and its predilection towards wonderfully bitter foods. Among these bitter foods is the bitter melon, which isn't a melon at all, but a wrinkly green gourd that more than lives up to its pungent name. Although bitter melon is indeed quite bitter, there is also a wonderful sweetness that follows its initial bite. This bittersweet flavor is one of the hallmarks of classic Ilocano dishes such as *pinakbet* (Stewed Vegetables with Pork Belly—page 49). My recipe for Bitter Melon and Bacon Quiche is a melding of an Ilocano breakfast favorite of scrambled eggs and bitter melon, and the classic French dish, *quiche* Lorraine. In my Franco-Filipino custard, the flavor of the bitter melon is complemented by the saltiness of bacon and the richness of cream and cheese.

Serves 8–10
Prep Time: 30 minutes
Cooking Time: 2 hours

1 recipe Flaky Pastry Pie Crust (page 23)
½ lb (250 g) bacon, cut into ¼-in (6-mm) thick matchsticks
1 cup (125 g) diced onion
1 cup (125 g) diced bitter melon (see How to Prepare Bitter Melon, opposite)
4 cloves garlic, minced
1 cup (70 g) shredded Edam cheese
3 large eggs, lightly beaten
1 cup (250 ml) milk
½ cup (125 ml) heavy cream
1 teaspoon fish sauce
½ teaspoon freshly ground black pepper

Roll out the dough for the Flaky Pastry Pie Crust on a lightly floured work surface, until the dough is 10–12 in (25–30 cm) in diameter. Fit the dough into a 9-in (23-cm) pie pan and trim the edges of the dough. Poke holes all over the dough with a fork, and then place the dough in the freezer to rest for 10–15 minutes—this rest time helps to prevent the dough from shrinking during baking.

Meanwhile, preheat the oven to 425°F (220°C).

Remove the chilled pie crust from the freezer. Line the pie crust with parchment paper or foil and fill with pie weights or dried beans to keep the crust flat while baking. Place the crust into the oven and bake for 15 minutes. Remove the weights and parchment paper and continue baking the crust until it is golden, 10–12 minutes more. Remove the crust from the oven and set aside to cool.

Reduce the oven temperature to 350°F (175°C).

Place the bacon in a large sauté pan over medium heat. Cook the bacon until brown and crisp, 5–7 minutes. Using a slotted spoon, transfer the bacon to a plate lined with a paper towel and set aside. Pour off all but 2 tablespoons of bacon fat from the pan and return the pan to medium heat.

Add the onion, bitter melon, and garlic to the pan and cook until the bitter melon is soft and tender, 5–7 minutes. Remove the pan from the heat and allow the vegetables to cool slightly.

Sprinkle half of the cheese over the bottom of the pre-baked pie crust, followed by half of the bacon and half of the vegetables, making sure that everything is evenly distributed. Layer in the rest of the cheese, followed by the remaining bacon and vegetables.

Whisk the eggs, milk, cream, fish sauce, and black pepper in a large bowl. Pour the egg mixture into the prepared piecrust. Place the *quiche* in the oven and bake until the center of the *quiche* is just set (it will still jiggle slightly), 35–40 minutes. Remove the *quiche* from the oven and allow to cool for at least 30 minutes before slicing and serving.

COOK'S NOTE: To save time, store-bought, pre-made refrigerated pie crust can be used for the *quiche* instead of making your own crust. Just follow the package instructions on how to pre-bake the crust, and then bake the *quiche* itself at 350°F (175°C).

HOW TO PREPARE BITTER MELON

1. Trim the ends of the bitter melon, and then slice it in half lengthwise.

2. Using a spoon or a melon baller, scrape out and discard the seeds and white pith from the center of the bitter melon.

3. Here's how your bitter melon should look once you've scooped out the pith.

4. Slice the bitter melon halves into thin or thick crescent shapes as needed, and then cut into chunks or small dice as needed.

KALE GREENS IN COCONUT MILK LYING LAING

Laing (pronounced "lah-ing") is conventionally made with fresh or dried *taro* leaves slowly simmered in coconut milk. But I've found that kale makes for a wonderfully hearty substitute for what I like to call "Lying *Laing*." Although the faux *laing* may initially upset Filipino food traditionalists, they won't be able to resist the deliciously tender kale in its spicy coconut broth.

I like the texture and bite of *lacinato* kale (also called Tuscan kale, or dinosaur kale), but any variety of kale works well in this recipe.

Serves 4–6
Prep Time: 15 minutes
Cooking Time: 25 minutes

2 tablespoons oil
1 onion, diced
4 cloves garlic, minced
1-in (2.5-cm) piece fresh ginger, peeled and minced
1–2 Thai chili peppers, split in half lengthwise with stems intact
1 tablespoon fermented shrimp paste
1 lb (500 g) kale, washed, center ribs and stems removed, leaves roughly chopped
½ cup (125 ml) Shrimp Stock (page 21), or water
1½ cups (375 ml) coconut milk
Salt, to taste
Freshly ground black pepper, to taste

Heat a large wok or sauté pan over high heat until a drop of water sizzles and evaporates on contact. Swirl the oil into the pan, and then add the onion and stir-fry until the pieces wilt and begin to lightly brown, 2–3 minutes.

Add the garlic, ginger, chili peppers, and shrimp paste to the pan and cook until fragrant, about 1 minute.

Toss the kale into the pan, and then cook and stir until the kale cooks down and wilts, 1–2 minutes.

Pour the Shrimp Stock and coconut milk into the pan and stir to combine. Bring to a boil, and then reduce heat to low and simmer, uncovered, until the kale is tender, 10–15 minutes. Season to taste with salt and black pepper. Serve with steamed white rice.

COOK'S NOTE: You can omit the shrimp paste and instead stir in 1 tablespoon of fish sauce when adding the coconut milk and water. Otherwise, you can season with additional salt.

BAKED EGGS WITH TOMATO, CHEESE AND FIRE-ROASTED EGGPLANT POQUI-POQUI

This is my interpretation of *poqui-poqui*—a Northern Filipino dish that features roasted eggplant sautéed with eggs and tomatoes to form a smoky eggplant scramble of sorts. Although I love the traditional *poqui-poqui*, I love runny egg yolks even more. By baking eggs in a ramekin of tomatoes, cheese and smoky eggplant, a runny yolk can be had to mix and mingle to my heart's content. This makes a light breakfast to be sure, but a breakfast layered with familiar Filipino flavors. Be sure to use the thin and slender purple Asian eggplant for this recipe, and not the large dark purple/black globe eggplant.

Serves 4
Prep Time: 10 minutes
Cooking Time: 35 minutes

1½ lbs (750 g) Asian eggplant, about 3–4 medium eggplants
1 tablespoon oil
1 tablespoon minced garlic
1 large tomato, diced
1 teaspoon fish sauce
½ teaspoon freshly ground black pepper
½ cup (35 g) shredded Edam cheese, or Gouda, or Swiss
4 large eggs
Soy sauce, to taste
Smoked Spanish paprika, or regular paprika, to taste

Pierce the eggplant all over with the tip of a sharp knife. Roast the eggplant directly over the gas flame of your stovetop, turning the eggplant with tongs to ensure the skin is charred on all sides, 5–7 minutes. Alternatively, you can place the eggplant on a cookie sheet directly under the broiler and broil, turning over once, until the skin is charred and wrinkled on all sides, 10–12 minutes total. The eggplant is done when the skin is charred and wrinkled, and the flesh is very soft. Set the charred eggplant aside to cool.

Preheat the oven to 400°F (200°C).

Meanwhile, heat the oil in a medium non-stick pan over moderately high heat. Add the garlic and cook until it just begins to brown, 2–3 minutes. Add the tomato, fish sauce, and black pepper and cook until the tomato softens and most of the juices have cooked away, 3–5 minutes. Remove the pan from the heat and set aside.

Cut off the eggplant caps and peel off the eggplant skins. Roughly chop the flesh of the eggplant, and then equally divide the flesh among four 1-cup (250-ml) oven-safe ramekins. Equally divide the shredded cheese among the ramekins, and then divide the tomato mixture among the ramekins.

Using the back of a spoon, form a shallow well in the center of each ramekin, and then crack an egg into each well—being careful not to break the yolks.

Place the ramekins onto a cookie sheet and bake in the oven until the egg whites are set, but the yolks are still runny, 15–20 minutes. Remove the ramekins from the oven. Drizzle each egg with soy sauce and season with paprika.

Serve the ramekins alone, or with *sinangag* (Fast and Simple Garlic Fried Rice—page 53) for a heartier breakfast.

COOK'S NOTE: The Ilocano dialect of the Philippines uses the term "*poqui-poqui*" in reference to their dish of eggplant, eggs and tomatoes. However, the Tagalog dialect of the Philippines has a very similar sounding term that doesn't reference a dish at all, but rather, um, lady parts. Which is why a dish of Ilocano *poqui-poqui* always garners a few giggles at the dinner table in other parts of the Philippines.

JICAMA, GREEN MANGO, AND GLASS NOODLE SALAD
ENSALADANG SINGKAMAS, MANGGA AT SOTANGHON

At first glance, a mish-mash of fresh *jicama*, sour green mangoes, and cold noodles may seem like a boring, if not unusual salad. At least that's what I thought when I first encountered this dish at my grandmother's dinner table some time ago.

But after one bite of the crisp and crunchy salad, I knew I had to have more. The seemingly simple mix of fish sauce, lime juice, pepper, and sugar create a wonderfully complex, yet balanced dressing for this cool refreshing salad—perfect for a hot summer day.

The salad is easier to eat when all of the veggies are cut into uniformly thin matchsticks—so if you've got a mandoline, this would be a great time to use it. If you don't have a mandoline, and would rather not spend the time cutting everything into thin matchsticks with your chef's knife, you can also cut the vegetables into more manageable bite-sized cubes—the salad will be just as delicious and refreshing no matter how the vegetables are cut.

Serves 4–6
Prep Time: 30 minutes

¼ lb (100 g) dried bean thread noodles (glass/cellophane noodles)
½ lb (250 g) *jicama*, peeled and cut into thin matchsticks
1 small firm green mango, peeled, deseeded and cut into thin matchsticks
1 small red bell pepper, deseeded and cut into thin matchsticks
1 small yellow bell pepper, deseeded and cut into thin matchsticks
2 green onions (scallions), trimmed and thinly sliced (white and green parts)
¼ cup (10 g) chopped fresh coriander leaves (cilantro)
2 tablespoons fish sauce
¼ cup (65 ml) fresh *calamansi* juice, or fresh lime juice
½ teaspoon freshly ground black pepper
2 tablespoons brown sugar

Using kitchen shears, cut the dried noodles into 3-in (7.5-cm) lengths. Soak the noodles in a medium bowl of hot water until soft. Drain the noodles into a fine mesh sieve, and then rinse the noodles with cold running water.

Place the drained noodles into a large bowl along with the *jicama*, mango, bell pepper, onion, and coriander leaves. Toss gently to combine. Refrigerate until ready to serve.

Combine the fish sauce, *calamansi* juice, black pepper, and brown sugar in a small bowl. Whisk until the sugar is completely dissolved.

Pour the dressing over the salad and toss gently to combine. Serve immediately.

STEWED VEGETABLES WITH PORK BELLY
PINAKBET

With sweet and tangy tomatoes, bitter melon, a touch of fish sauce and a smattering of pork belly, all of the five tastes—sweet, sour, bitter, salty and *umami*—harmonize in the rustic Filipino stew of *pinakbet*. Like most other Filipino dishes, there is more than one way to make *pinakbet* since a range of different vegetables can be added to the pot. But to make a really great *pinakbet*, use only the best tomatoes you can find as they will impart a great deal of flavor and liquid to the stew. A secret I learned from my Great Auntie Puyong (AKA Grandma Puyong) is to first toss and mix all of the ingredients in the pot so that everything is coated in the fish sauce and the juice of the chopped tomatoes. This "secret" step keeps the tender vegetables intact during cooking, as no stirring is needed. This is my version of my Great Auntie Puyong's *pinakbet*—my favorite dish in the world.

Serves 6–8
Prep Time: 15 minutes
Cooking Time: 25 minutes

4 large, ripe tomatoes, roughly chopped
¼ cup (65 ml) fish sauce, plus more, to taste
6–8 cloves garlic, pressed with the side of a knife and peeled
1 large onion, sliced
1 lb (500 g) Asian eggplant, halved lengthwise and cut into ½-in (1.25-cm) chunks
½ lb (250 g) long beans, trimmed and cut into 2-in (5-cm) pieces
1 large bitter melon, cut into 1-in (2.5-cm) chunks (see How to Prepare Bitter Melon, page 45)
½ lb (250 g) Crunchy Pork Belly (page 89), cut into bite-sized pieces (see Cook's Notes)

Add all of the ingredients, and half of the fried pork belly (*lechon kawali*), to a large deep pot. Using your hands, gently toss everything in the pot so that all the ingredients are coated in the liquid from the fish sauce and chopped tomatoes.

Place the pot over high heat and bring to a boil. Reduce the heat to moderately-low, and then cover and simmer for 15 minutes without stirring. Layer the remaining pork belly on top of the stew and continue to simmer for another 5 minutes.

Taste the soup that has accumulated in the bottom of the pot. Season with additional fish sauce if desired. The vegetables should be tender and *al dente* when finished. Simmer for 5 more minutes if the vegetables are not done to your liking. Serve with steamed white rice.

> **COOK'S NOTES:** If you choose not to make your own *lechon kawali* (page 89), you can find freshly fried pork belly at Asian and Latin markets. The pork can also be left out of the dish altogether for a vegetarian *pinakbet*.
>
> If you'd rather not use bitter melon, you can substitute an equal amount of zucchini—just don't serve it to my Grandma Puyong!
>
> For a less soupy *pinakbet*, reduce the amount of tomatoes and fish sauce by half.

CHAPTER 3

SOUPS, NOODLES, AND RICE
SABAW, PANCIT AT KANIN

The sheer diversity of Filipino cuisine can perhaps best be seen in its array of different soup, noodle, and rice dishes.

Although Filipino soups are often swimming with an assortment of vegetables and a range of meats, poultry, or seafood, they are often served with the rest of the meal rather than as a separate course. And because steamed white rice acts as a culinary sponge, soaking up whatever flavors are paired with it, common Filipino practice is to eat soup with rice—I like to place a scoop of rice into the bottom of my soup bowl before ladling the soup on top.

While *pancit* noodles are derived directly from the Chinese, Filipinos have taken the starchy strands and run with them—creating a variety of noodle dishes that are either quickly stir-fried or even simmered into soups, all of which are appointed with different sauces, gravies, meats, and vegetables.

And whether simply steamed, fried, or cooked into a soul-satisfying porridge, rice is undoubtedly king of the Filipino meal.

With such a wide breadth and depth of soup, noodle, and rice dishes from the Philippines, an entire book can be filled with those recipes alone. Luckily, I've provided just a selection of my favorites here. Enjoy, and slurp loudly.

COCONUT MILK RISOTTO WITH SQUASH AND LONG BEANS

Much like my inspiration for Roasted *Kabocha* Squash Soup (page 60), this *risotto* recipe also sprouted from a standard Filipino dish called *ginataang kalabasa at sitaw* that features squash and long beans cooked in coconut milk and served over steamed rice. But rather than simmering the vegetables in coconut milk, the long beans are quickly blanched, and the sweet *kabocha* squash is grated and cooked slowly with the *risotto* rice grains. Finally, the *risotto* is enriched and bolstered with coconut milk. Containing all of the necessary ingredients for *ginataang kalabasa at sitaw*, this creamy *risotto* is essentially the same dish, just presented in a very different way.

Serves 4–6
Prep Time: 15 minutes
Cooking Time: 45 minutes

4 cups (1 liter) homemade Chicken Stock (page 21), or store-bought chicken stock
¼ lb (100 g) long beans, trimmed and cut into 2-in (5-cm) pieces
2 tablespoons oil
1 tablespoon butter
1 onion, diced
One 1-in (2.5-cm) piece peeled and finely minced fresh ginger
2 cloves garlic, finely minced
1 cup (200 g) *Arborio* rice
1 cup (70 g) grated *kabocha* squash
½ cup (125 ml) dry white wine
1 tablespoon fish sauce
½ cup (125 ml) canned unsweetened coconut milk, plus more for drizzling
Salt, to taste
Freshly ground black pepper, to taste

Pour the Chicken Stock into a medium saucepan over high heat and bring to a boil. Add the long beans to the boiling stock and cook until the beans are slightly tender and bright green, about 2 minutes. Using a slotted spoon, transfer the beans to a large bowl filled with ice water to stop the beans from cooking further. Drain the beans and set aside. Reduce the heat to low and cover the chicken stock—you will continue to use this stock throughout the recipe.

On a separate burner from the stock, heat the oil and butter in a large saucepan over medium heat. Add the onion and cook until soft and translucent, 5–7 minutes. Add the ginger and garlic and cook until the garlic just begins to brown, 2–3 minutes. Stir in the rice to coat all the grains in the oil and butter and cook until the grains just begin to toast, about 5 minutes.

Add the grated squash, pour in the white wine and reduce the heat to medium low, stirring frequently until the rice has absorbed most of the wine. Add the fish sauce and about 1 cup (250 ml) of the warm chicken stock to the rice and stir until the liquid is almost absorbed.

Continue adding the stock, a ladleful at a time, stirring frequently and allowing each addition of stock to absorb before adding the next. This process of adding stock will take about 20–30 minutes over moderately-low to low heat, wherein you may or may not use all of the chicken stock. If you find that you've used all of the chicken stock and the rice is still hard, continue adding water to the rice in place of the chicken stock.

After 20 minutes of cooking, start checking the doneness of the rice. The rice grains should be tender but slightly firm in the center and the *risotto* should have a loose, creamy consistency. After the rice has reached the right texture, stir in the coconut milk and the reserved long beans and cook just until the long beans are warmed through, about 1 minute more.

Taste the *risotto* and season with the salt and black pepper as needed. Divide the *risotto* into individual servings and drizzle each serving with more coconut milk if desired. Serve immediately.

FAST AND SIMPLE GARLIC FRIED RICE
SINANGAG

Serves 4–6
Prep Time: 5 minutes
Cooking Time: 10 minutes

4 cups (650 g) cold leftover steamed white rice
2 tablespoons high-heat cooking oil
6–8 cloves garlic, smashed with the side of a knife and peeled
1 teaspoon coarse salt, plus more, to taste

When I was a young child, the best part about spending the night at my grandparents' house was waking up to the smell of sizzling garlic in the morning. I'd stumble out of bed and follow the aroma to the kitchen, where I'd find my Great Auntie Puyong conjuring at the stove. "You want *kinirog?*" she'd ask, using the Ilocano word for garlic fried rice. I'd nod my head yes, and hop on over to the table to wait for my breakfast. And like magic, my Auntie Puyong transformed the previous days' rice into something entirely different and special to be eaten as part of a hearty break-fast. As I learned from my Auntie Puyong (AKA Grandma Puyong), the secret to a great fried rice is to simply use cold leftover rice from the previous day. I like to spread cooked steamed rice onto a large platter or baking sheet in a very thin layer. I then refrigerate the rice overnight, uncovered. The next morning, the rice will be dried out and any sticky clumps can be easily broken apart and ready for a hot pan.

Using a wet rice paddle or wooden spoon, gently break apart any large clumps of rice that may be sticking together. Set the rice aside.

Heat a large wok or sauté pan over high heat until a drop of water sizzles and evaporates on contact. Swirl the oil into the pan and then add the garlic and stir-fry until the garlic begins to lightly brown, 30 seconds to 1 minute.

Add the rice to the pan and quickly toss and mix with the garlic and oil, breaking up any remaining clumps of rice with a spatula. Sprinkle in the salt and continue to stir-fry until the rice is coated in oil and lightly toasted, about 5 minutes. Season the rice with additional salt if needed. Serve hot.

FILIPINO BREAKFAST [AND WORDPLAY]

The fact that breakfast is the most important meal of the day is not lost on Filipinos. Morning time meals are very often hearty affairs that can resemble multi-course feasts. Even thick rice porridges like *champorado* (Chocolate and Coffee Rice Pudding—page 135) and *arroz caldo* (Chicken and Rice Porridge—page 54) are frequently eaten for breakfast. The most common breakfast items though, are usually garlic fried rice, fried eggs, and a protein of choice that can range from sausage, to dried fish, to even Spam. Because garlic fried rice and fried eggs are always paired together for breakfast, dishes that contain the two items are more commonly known as *"silogs."* The word *"silog"* is a combination of the Filipino words for garlic fried rice: *"sinangag,"* and eggs: *"itlog."* And depending on what protein is served with the rice and eggs, an identifier is added to the –*silog* suffix. So for example, a breakfast of Filipino Garlic Sausage Patties (*longganisa*—page 93) served together with garlic fried rice and fried eggs would be called *"longsilog."* Likewise, Glazed Roasted Spam (page 92), rice and eggs would be *"spamsilog,"* and there is even *"tofusilog," "chixsilog,"* and *"adobosilog"* among many, many others. This goes to show that Filipinos are just as creative with their words as they are with their food.

CHICKEN AND RICE PORRIDGE
ARROZ CALDO

People find solace in comfort foods for different reasons. Sometimes, when certain flavors, textures, and aromas are evocative of a certain time or place, it's entirely possible to find happiness in a bowl. For me, a bowl of *arroz caldo* often conjures memories of the holidays and of family. Every year on Christmas Eve, without fail, my mother has a pot of the thick porridge simmering away on her stove. The smells of chicken, and rice, and garlic, and ginger, and fish sauce all waft throughout the house as the pot slowly simmers. Enjoying a simple, yet flavorful porridge of chicken and rice has become such a rich tradition, that I now make *arroz caldo* for my wife and son every New Year's Eve. The *arroz caldo* I make is slightly different than my mom's—I fry the skins from the chicken thighs to make crispy chicken cracklings to add extra crunch and flavor to the finished porridge.

Serves 6–8
Prep Time: 15 minutes
Cooking Time: 1 hour

2 lbs (1 kg) skin-on, bone-in chicken thighs
1 tablespoon oil
Salt, to taste
Freshly ground black pepper, to taste
1 tablespoon minced garlic
1 large onion, thinly sliced
One 3-in (7.5-cm) piece peeled fresh ginger, cut into thin matchsticks
4 tablespoons fish sauce
2 cups (500 g) uncooked medium-grain rice
8 cups (2 liters) water
1 teaspoon freshly ground black pepper

For garnish:
2 green onions (scallions), trimmed and thinly sliced (white and green parts)
Calamansi limes, cut in half (or lemon wedges)
Additional fish sauce

Using your hands, gently remove the skin from the chicken thighs. With a little bit of effort, you should be able to pull off the skin from each thigh in one piece. Pat the chicken skins dry with paper towels and set aside.

Heat the oil in a large pot or Dutch oven over moderately high heat. Lay the chicken skins flat, with the fat side down (the smooth side of the skin), into the pot. Press on the chicken skins with a spatula to keep them the first side becomes brown and crispy, about 5 minutes. Flip the skins over and continue frying until the second side is brown and crispy, 3–5 minutes.

Transfer the crisped chicken skins to a plate lined with paper towels. Season the cracklings with salt and pepper and set aside for garnish.

Pour off all but 1 tablespoon of fat from the pot. Add the garlic to the pot and fry until golden brown and crisp, 2–3 minutes. Transfer the garlic to a plate lined with a paper towel and set aside for garnish.

Add the onion and ginger to the remaining oil in the pot and cook until the onion becomes soft and translucent, 3–5 minutes. Add the chicken thighs and fish sauce to the pot and stir to combine. Place the lid on the pot, reduce the heat to moderately-low and cook for about 5 minutes, until the chicken meat just begins to turn white and releases some of its juices.

Uncover the pot and add the uncooked rice, stirring until the rice absorbs most of the liquid in the pot, 2–3 minutes. Pour the water into the pot and bring to a boil over high heat. Reduce the heat to moderately-low, and then simmer uncovered for 20 minutes, stirring occasionally.

Remove the chicken thighs from the pot and set aside to cool. Once cool enough to handle, remove the chicken meat from the bones, and then shred the chicken meat and discard the bones. Add the shredded chicken meat back into the pot and stir in the 1 teaspoon of black pepper.

The porridge will thicken as the rice cooks and absorbs liquid. If the porridge becomes too thick after 30 minutes of simmering, more water can be added. If the porridge isn't thick enough, continue simmering until it reaches the desired consistency.

Spoon the porridge into bowls and garnish with the crispy chicken cracklings, fried garlic and green onion. Serve with the *calamansi* limes (or lemon wedges) and additional fish sauce on the side.

MUNG BEAN STEW WITH BACON AND SPINACH BALATONG

Balatong (also known as *mongo guisado*) is a hearty and simple Filipino stew of mung beans, tomatoes, and greens. Ironically, I crave this warm stew the most during winter months, when fresh tomatoes are out of season. But I've found that a can of diced tomatoes is a great remedy for bland out-of-season tomatoes. Though *balatong* can be made as a vegetarian dish, it is normally studded with either shrimp, pork, or both. My updated version of *balatong* uses bacon—a new twist that I'm sure even the staunchest of *balatong* fans will enjoy. One such fan is my older brother. He was so fond of *balatong* when we were younger, that he earned the nickname "Oohjong Balatong." Although "Bacon Balatong" doesn't quite sound as silly, it still has a nice ring to it. Bacon tends to have that effect on things.

Serves 4–6
Prep Time: 15 minutes
Cooking Time: 1 hour, 45 minutes

½ lb (250 g) bacon, finely chopped
1 large onion, chopped
4 cloves garlic, minced
1 cup (250 g) dried mung beans, rinsed
One 14.5-oz (410-g) can diced tomatoes
6 cups (1.5 liters) water
2 tablespoons fish sauce, plus more, to taste
Salt, to taste
Freshly ground black pepper, to taste
1 bunch fresh spinach, washed and stems trimmed

Cook the bacon in a large, deep pot or Dutch oven over medium heat until the bacon is brown and crisp, 5–7 minutes. Using a slotted spoon, transfer the bacon bits to a small plate lined with a paper towel. Set the bacon bits aside. Pour off all but 1 tablespoon of bacon fat from the pot and return the pot to medium heat.

Add the onion and garlic to the pot and cook until the onion becomes soft and translucent, 5–7 minutes. Add the mung beans and stir to combine, cooking for 1–2 minutes more so that the mung beans absorb some of the oil in the pot. Pour in the tomatoes, water, and fish sauce, stirring to scrape up any browned bits from the bottom of the pot.

Increase the heat to high and bring the pot to a boil. Cover the pot, reduce the heat to low and simmer until the mung beans are soft and tender, 1 hour to 1 hour, 30 minutes. If the stew becomes too thick before the mung beans have softened, add more water as needed.

Taste the stew and season with salt and pepper and additional fish sauce if desired. Stir in the spinach—depending on the size of your pot, you may have to add the spinach in batches. Continue to cook over low heat until all of the spinach softens and wilts down.

Serve the stew in individual bowls and garnish with the reserved bacon bits.

> **COOK'S NOTE:** For a more traditional *balatong*, omit the bacon and sauté the onion and garlic in vegetable oil. Then stir in some chopped *lechon kawali* (Crunchy Pork Belly—page 89) and simmer the stew as directed. You can also choose to use Shrimp Stock (page 21) instead of water, as well as add peeled and deveined raw shrimp to the stew. For a thicker *balatong*, uncover the stew as it simmers. Allow it to simmer until the mung beans become tender and the stew becomes as thick as you'd like.

PORK AND SHRIMP DUMPLING SOUP PANCIT MOLO

Named after the Molo District in Iloilo City of the Philippines, *pancit* Molo features pork and shrimp dumplings simmered in a clear chicken stock. In other words, *panict* Molo is wonton soup—a very obvious connection to the Chinese influence in Filipino cuisine. In fact, during Spanish colonial times, a large population of Chinese lived and worked in the Molo District, many of whom made their living hawking wonton soup. Although we might be familiar with the term "*pancit*" generally referring to noodles, wonton dumplings also fall under the *pancit* category in the same way that ravioli and spaghetti are both classified as pasta. Because these dumplings freeze well, it makes sense to make a large batch so that you can easily make multiple iterations of the soup in the future by simply dropping some of the frozen wontons into the hot chicken stock.

Serves 4–6 as part of a multi-course meal
Prep Time: 1 hour
Cooking Time: 30 minutes

For the dumplings:
(Makes about 60–65 dumplings)
65 store-bought wonton wrappers
1 lb (500 g) ground pork
½ lb (250 g) peeled and deveined raw
   shrimp, minced
1 teaspoon cornstarch
1 teaspoon salt
1 teaspoon freshly ground black pepper
One 1-in (2.5-cm) piece peeled and
   finely minced fresh ginger
1 large egg, beaten

For the soup:
1 tablespoon oil
1 small onion, chopped
4–6 cloves garlic, minced
6 cups (1.5 liters) homemade Chicken
   Stock (page 21), or store-bought
   chicken stock
2 tablespoons fish sauce, plus more, to
   taste
½ teaspoon freshly ground black
   pepper, plus more, to taste
24 pork and shrimp dumplings
2 green onions (scallions), thinly sliced
   (white and green parts)

To make the dumplings, remove the wonton wrappers from their packaging and place them underneath a damp paper towel to prevent them from drying out. Place the rest of the dumpling ingredients in a large bowl and gently mix until thoroughly combined. To form the dumplings, see the illustrated instructions to the right.

To make the soup, heat the oil in a large pot over moderately high heat. Add the onion and sauté until soft and translucent, 3–5 minutes. Add the garlic and cook until the garlic just begins to brown, 2–3 minutes. Pour in the chicken stock, stirring to scrape up any browned bits from the bottom of the pot. Stir in the fish sauce and the black pepper, increase the heat to high and bring the stock to a boil.

Gently add 24 of the pork and shrimp dumplings to the pot, and then cover and simmer over low heat until the dumplings are cooked through, 10–15 minutes. Taste the soup and add more fish sauce and black pepper as needed. Garnish with the green onion and serve immediately.

HOW TO FILL AND FOLD THE PANCIT MOLO DUMPLINGS

1. Place 1 wonton wrapper on a clean, dry work surface so that one corner of the wrapper is pointing at you (positioned like a diamond, rather than a square).

2. Place 1 teaspoon of the filling just under the midpoint of the diamond, closest to the corner pointing at you.

3. Take the corner closest to you and roll it up and over the filling.

4. Continue to roll the wrapper until about half of the wrapper remains in contact with the work surface.

5. Using a wet finger, press down and moisten the left and right corners of the wrapper.

6. Fold the left and right corners of the wrapper up and over the filling.

7. Place the finished dumplings aside, underneath a moist towel, and continue rolling until all of the filling has been used.

To freeze the dumplings, place them in a single layer on a baking sheet and place in the freezer until completely frozen. Transfer the frozen dumplings to a large resealable food storage bag and store in the freezer for up to 3 months.

SHRIMP AND PORK WITH HOMEMADE PANCIT NOODLES
PANCIT MIKI

Pancit miki is one of my family's most revered and favorite dishes, yet only one person in my family makes it—my Great Auntie Carling (AKA Grandma Carling). Although *miki* is usually only made for special occasions, my Grandma Carling makes this homemade noodle dish upon request—which is often. And despite being in her late 80s, my Grandma Carling can still crank out the *miki* with the speed and efficiency of Manny Pacquiao. *Pancit miki* features rustic homemade noodles swimming in a sauce laden with the flavors of ginger and garlic, pork belly, and shrimp. Although served "soupy" with lots of sauce, it really isn't fair to call *miki* a soup, as it has the consistency and richness of a chowder—but without having any cream. The secret is in the homemade noodles, whose dusting of flour helps to thicken the flavorful sauce. If you don't have the time to make your own noodles, you can find fresh *miki* noodles in the refrigerator section of the Asian market, but store-bought noodles won't thicken the sauce the way homemade noodles will. Luckily, you don't have to be a prizefighter, or a Filipino grandmother, to make your own *pancit miki* noodles. All it takes is a little flour, water, and oil. This is my version of *pancit miki*, with just a few changes to my Grandma Carling's recipe—I can't give up all of my family secrets, can I?

Serves 6–8
Prep Time: 40 minutes
Cooking Time: 30 minutes

For the noodles:
2 cups (275 g) all-purpose flour, plus more for rolling and dusting the dough
1 tablespoon Annatto Oil (page 26), or regular vegetable oil
¾ cup (185 ml) water, divided

For the sauce:
2 tablespoons Annatto Oil (page 26), or regular vegetable oil
1 lb (500 g) pork belly, cut into ¼-in (6-mm) chunks
1 large onion, diced
6 cloves garlic, minced
One 2-in (5-cm) piece fresh ginger, peeled and minced
4 cups (1 liter) Shrimp Stock (page 21)
1 cup (250 ml) water
¼ cup (65 ml) fish sauce, plus more, to taste
1 lb (500 g) fresh or previously frozen medium shrimp, peeled and deveined
Salt, to taste
Freshly ground black pepper, to taste
2 green onions (scallions), trimmed and thinly sliced (white and green parts)
Fresh *calamansi* limes, or lemon wedges, for squeezing over the noodles

To make the noodles, combine the flour, oil, and only a ½ cup (125 ml) of the water in a large bowl. Mix the ingredients together with a rubber spatula until all of the liquid is incorporated into the flour. Add the remaining ¼ cup (65 ml) of the water, a tablespoon at a time, until a dough comes together and forms a ball. You may not have to use all of the water. The dough should hold its shape and be slightly sticky, but not overly wet.

Place the dough on a lightly floured work surface. Knead the dough with both hands by pushing the dough down and away from you with the heel of your palms. Fold the dough back onto itself, rotate it and continue kneading. If the dough becomes sticky, sprinkle more flour over it. Continue kneading the dough for at least another

5 minutes, stretching it out in front of you, folding it back onto itself, rotating it and repeating the kneading while adding more flour as needed. The dough will soon become smooth and supple and less sticky. It is important to knead the dough in order to develop and stretch the gluten within it, thereby strengthening the dough and making for a firmer noodle.

To form the noodles from the dough, follow the illustrated instructions to the right.

To make the sauce, you will need a large wok or deep pot that can accommodate a large amount of noodles and sauce.

Heat the large wok or deep pot over high heat until a drop of water sizzles and evaporates on contact. Swirl the oil into the pot, and then add the pork belly and onion. Stir-fry until the pork begins to brown around the edges and the onion begins to soften, 2–3 minutes. Add the garlic and ginger and cook until the garlic just begins to brown, 1–2 minutes. Pour in the Shrimp Stock, water, and fish sauce, stirring to scrape up any browned bits from the bottom of the pot, and bring to a boil.

Gently add the noodles to the pot, stirring to prevent the noodles from clumping together. Return the liquid to a boil, and then reduce the heat to moderately-low and simmer for 10 minutes, stirring frequently. Stir in the shrimp and continue cooking until the shrimp are just cooked through and the sauce has thickened, about 5 minutes. Taste the sauce and adjust the seasoning with salt and pepper, or more fish sauce if desired. The sauce will continue to thicken as the *miki* sits.

Garnish the *miki* with the green onion and serve immediately with *calamansi* limes or lemon wedges on the side.

> **COOK'S NOTES:** If you have an electric stand mixer, you can speed up the noodle-making by forming and kneading the dough with the mixer. You can also use a manual or electric pasta maker to roll and cut the noodles.
> You can make *pancit miki* with chicken instead of pork and shrimp, and you can use Chicken Stock (page 21) in place of the Shrimp Stock.

HOW TO ROLL AND CUT THE PANCIT MIKI NOODLES

1. Place your ball of *miki* dough on a lightly floured work surface.

2. Form the dough into a cylinder, and then gently press and roll the dough with your palms to stretch it into a 12-in (30-cm) long log. Use a knife to divide the log into two 6-in (15-cm) pieces.

3. Cut each log into 4 equal pieces to yield 8 pieces of dough total.

4. Using a rolling pin, roll each of the dough pieces until they are roughly 1/8-in (3-mm) thick by 5 in (13 cm) in diameter.

5. Dust the discs of dough with flour to keep them from sticking, and then cut the discs of dough into 1/4-in (6-mm) strips, and then cut the strips in half.

6. After cutting all of the noodles, dust with additional flour to ensure that they don't stick to each other and set aside underneath a moist towel until ready to use.

ROASTED KABOCHA SQUASH SOUP

The inspiration for this soup comes from a traditional Filipino dish known as *ginataang kalabasa* that features squash simply simmered in coconut milk. I decided to take things a little further by adding a few more flavors in the form of ginger and citrus, and then puréeing everything with a blender for a completely new and luscious soup with familiar flavors.

Serves 4–6 as part of a multi-course meal
Prep Time: 10 minutes
Cooking Time: 2 hours

1 small *kabocha* squash, about 2 lbs (1 kg) total
Salt, to taste
Freshly ground black pepper, to taste
2 tablespoons oil
1 onion, diced
2 cloves garlic, minced
One 1-in (2.5-cm) piece fresh ginger, peeled and minced
1½ cups (375 ml) Shrimp Stock (page 21)
1 cup (250 ml) coconut milk, plus more for garnish
2 teaspoons sugar
2 tablespoons fish sauce
1 tablespoon fresh *calamansi* juice, or fresh lime juice
Fresh coriander leaves (cilantro), for garnish

Preheat the oven to 375°F (190°C). Line a sheet pan with foil or parchment paper.

Cut the squash in half and remove the seeds. Season each half with salt and pepper, and then place each half, cut side down, on the prepared sheet pan. Roast the squash in the oven until it is soft and a paring knife can be easily inserted into the flesh, 1 to 1½ hours. Remove the squash from the oven and set aside to cool.

Meanwhile, heat the oil in a large saucepan over moderately high heat. Add the onion, garlic, and ginger, and cook until the onion becomes soft and translucent, 5–7 minutes. Pour in the Shrimp Stock and coconut milk, stirring to scrape up any browned bits from the bottom of the pan. Using a spoon, scoop the flesh of the roasted squash from the skin and into the pan. Discard the squash skins.

Stir the sugar and fish sauce into the pan, increase the heat to high, and bring the soup to a boil. Reduce the heat to low and simmer for 10 minutes. Remove from the heat and stir in the *calamansi* juice.

Using an immersion blender, purée the soup until smooth. Alternatively, you can purée the soup in batches in the carafe of a blender. If the soup is too thick for your liking, you can add more Shrimp Stock or water to thin it out. Taste the soup for seasoning, and add more salt and pepper as needed.

Divide the soup into individual bowls, and then drizzle with coconut milk and garnish with fresh coriander leaves. Serve warm.

COOK'S NOTES: After blending the soup, you can add ½ lb (250 g) of peeled and deveined raw shrimp and simmer the soup until the shrimp are cooked through. *Voila!* Shrimp and *kabocha* squash bisque.

For a completely vegan soup, substitute water or vegetable stock for the Shrimp Stock, omit the fish sauce and season with salt.

STIR-FRIED WHEAT FLOUR NOODLES WITH SHRIMP AND VEGETABLES
PANCIT CANTON

Pancit Canton is as versatile as it is flavorful. Use the recipe here as a template, but feel free to improvise or change the vegetables and protein based on what is available in your kitchen.

For instance, although the recipe here specifies that the dried noodles soak in Shrimp Stock (page 21), you can also use homemade Chicken Stock (page 21) or store-bought chicken stock depending on your preferences. After absorbing the flavors of shrimp or chicken stock, the noodles can then be quickly stir-fried with any variety of vegetables, as well as embellished with any combination of meat, including shrimp, chicken, or pork.

Serves 4 as part of a multi-course meal
Prep Time: 15 minutes
Cooking Time: 15 minutes

8 oz (250 g) dried Canton noodles
1 cup (250 ml) Shrimp Stock (page 21)
1 tablespoon fish sauce
1 tablespoon soy sauce
1 tablespoon oyster sauce
1 tablespoon high-heat cooking oil
1 small onion, sliced
6 cloves garlic, minced
1 cup (75 g) grated carrot
1 lb (500 g) raw medium shrimp, peeled and deveined
2 cups (100 g) roughly chopped baby *bok choy*
1 cup (75 g) mung bean sprouts
1 teaspoon freshly ground black pepper
Calamansi limes, halved, or lemon wedges, for squeezing
Sriracha hot sauce (optional)

Place the dried noodles in a large bowl.

Combine the Shrimp Stock, fish sauce, soy sauce, and oyster sauce in a small pot over high heat and bring to a boil. As soon as the liquid boils, remove it from the heat and pour it over the dried noodles in the bowl. Gently toss the noodles until they absorb most of the liquid and begin to soften. At first glance, it may not seem like there is enough liquid to soften the noodles, but remain patient and continue to toss the noodles and they will eventually become tender. Set the bowl of noodles aside.

Heat a large wok or sauté pan over high heat until a drop of water sizzles and evaporates on contact. Swirl the oil into the pan, and then add the onion and stir-fry until the pieces soften and begin to lightly brown, 2–3 minutes. Add the garlic and carrot, and cook until the garlic just begins to brown, 1–2 minutes.

Toss in the shrimp and the baby *bok choy* and cook until the shrimp just begin to turn pink, 1–2 minutes. Add the softened noodles, along with any liquid left in the bowl, to the pan. Add the mung bean sprouts and the black pepper and toss to combine. Continue to toss and stir-fry everything in the pan until the shrimp are cooked through, 3–5 minutes more.

Serve with *calamansi* lime halves, or lemon wedges, on the side for squeezing over the *pancit*. For extra spice, a squirt of Sriracha hot sauce is a welcome addition over the noodles as well.

BEEF SHORT RIB SOUR SOUP SINIGANG NA BAKA

This version of *sinigang* employs a long, gentle simmer of bone-in beef short ribs to create a rich and flavorful broth. To sour the broth, either *tamarind* concentrate or *tamarind* pulp (see page 18 for more information on *tamarind*) can be used. If you can't locate any *tamarind*, you can instead increase the amount of *calamansi* or lemon juice in the recipe to suit your tastes. The sourness of the broth is balanced with a bit of heat supplied by mild chili peppers, and bursts of sweetness from cherry tomatoes. Thinly sliced *taro* root and chopped *bok choy* lend additional texture to the tender short ribs. This is indeed a full-flavored and robust beef *sinigang*.

Serves 4–6
Prep Time: 15 minutes
Cooking Time: 2 hours, 15 minutes

SINIGANG: A SOULFUL SOUR SOUP

Although *adobo* is widely considered to be the national dish of the Philippines, it can be argued that *sinigang*, the Filipino sour soup, deserves equal recognition. Like *adobo*, *sinigang* exists in a variety of incarnations across the Philippines. The clear broth soup can contain any variety of meats, poultry and seafood, and is typically studded with a variety of local vegetables. And like Chinese hot and sour soup (made with vinegar), or like Thai *tom yum* soup (made with lime juice and lime leaves), *sinigang* has a mouth-puckering tartness to it—but that tartness is achieved in a different way. Depending on the region, a range of native fruits can be used to give *sinigang* its trademark tang. And although vinegar is a vital ingredient in Filipino cooking, it is never used as a souring agent for *sinigang*. The typical souring agents that can be used include unripe *tamarind* pods and leaves, *kamias* (a very sour green fruit pod native to the Philippines), guava, starfruit, tomatoes, as well as *calamansi* and *dayap* (another variety of Philippine lime). Although green *tamarind* is difficult to come by in other parts of the world, *tamarind* concentrate and *tamarind* pulp can be found at many Asian markets. In addition, artificially flavored *tamarind* powder, sold in foil packets and more widely available, can also be used to make *sinigang* (see page 18 for more information on *tamarind*).

And of course, lemon juice is a perfectly acceptable souring agent in any *sinigang*. Whatever souring agent you choose, always keep in mind that each diner has a different preference for sourness. So it is perfectly acceptable, if not outright customary, to serve *sinigang* with a side of lemon wedges (or *calamansi* if you've got it) and additional fish sauce so that each diner can adjust the soup to his or her liking.

2 tablespoons oil
3 lbs (1.5 kg) beef short ribs
Salt, to taste
Freshly ground black pepper, to taste
4 cloves garlic, smashed with the side of a knife and peeled
8 cups (1.75 liters) water
1 cup (250 ml) *tamarind* concentrate, or 3 oz (75 g) *tamarind* pulp soaked in 1 cup (250 ml) of hot water and strained
¼ cup (65 ml) fresh *calamansi* juice, or fresh lemon juice
2 tablespoons fish sauce
1 onion, sliced
2 mild yellow chili peppers
1 lb (500 g) cherry tomatoes, halved
1 lb (500 g) small fresh *taro* root, peeled, cut in half lengthwise and sliced into thin half-moon shapes.
3–4 stalks (stems and leaves) *bok choy*, cut into 1-in (2.5-cm) chunks, or 3 heads of baby *bok choy*, chopped

Heat the oil in a large pot or Dutch oven over moderately high heat. Season the short ribs on all sides with the salt and freshly ground black pepper, and then add the short ribs to the pot in batches. Cook the short ribs until brown on all sides, 3–5 minutes per side. Transfer the short ribs to a large platter and set aside.

Pour off all but 1 tablespoon of fat from the pot, and then return the pot to medium heat. Add the garlic and sauté until the garlic just begins to brown, 1–2 minutes. Pour in the water, stirring to scrape up any browned bits from the bottom of the pot.

Return the short ribs, and any accumulated juices from the platter, to the pot and increase the heat to high. Bring the pot to a boil. Reduce the heat to low, and then cover and simmer for 1 hour, occasionally skimming and discarding any foam or fat that rises to the surface of the liquid.

After simmering the short ribs for 1 hour, stir in the *tamarind* concentrate (or *tamarind*-steeped water, if using), *calamansi* juice (or lemon juice, if using), and fish sauce. Drop in the onion, chili peppers, tomatoes and *taro* root and continue to simmer for 1 hour more, or until the meat is very tender and falling from the bones. Stir in the *bok choy* and simmer until tender, 3–5 minutes.

Taste the soup and add more of the *calamansi* (or lemon) juice if more sourness is desired. Season with additional fish sauce as needed. Serve with steamed white rice on the side.

FILIPINO SPAGHETTI

Pancit aren't the only noodles loudly slurped by Filipinos. Filipinos also love spaghetti. More specifically, Filipinos love spaghetti with a sweet tomato sauce mixed with banana ketchup and studded with sliced hot dogs. While the idea of spaghetti with a sugary ketchup sauce and sliced frankfurters can sound strange, it's actually a wonderful melding of sweet, salty, and tangy. Although the tasty reasons for the Filipino love of spaghetti are clear, the origins of the dish remain a bit murky. Some credit Italian-American GI's with introducing spaghetti and meat sauce to the Philippines; the spaghetti was then adapted to suit the sweet-toothed Filipino palate. However, it's more likely that the Japanese brought a similar dish called "spaghetti Napolitan" to the Philippines during their WWII occupation there. No matter how, or from where, spaghetti was introduced to the Philippines, the sweet Filipino rendition of the Italian pasta has become beloved throughout the islands. The sweet pasta dish is so popular that it is often served everywhere from fast food restaurants to children's birthday parties. My version of Filipino Spaghetti—with bacon and red wine, in addition to the hot dogs and banana ketchup—is sure to please kids and grown-ups alike.

Serves 4–6
Prep Time: 15 minutes
Cooking Time: 45 minutes

4 oz (100 g) bacon (about 4 strips), finely chopped
4 hot dogs, cut on the diagonal into ¼-in (6-mm) thick slices
½ lb (250 g) ground beef
1 teaspoon salt
1 teaspoon freshly ground black pepper
1 onion, diced
1 green bell pepper, diced
4 cloves garlic, minced
¼ teaspoon dried red pepper flakes
2 tablespoons tomato paste
1 cup (250 ml) red wine
½ cup (125 ml) Homemade Banana Ketchup (page 24), or store-bought banana ketchup
One 14.5-oz (410-g) can crushed tomatoes
1 tablespoon fish sauce
1 teaspoon dried oregano
1 tablespoon brown sugar, plus more to taste
1 lb (500 g) dried spaghetti
Fresh parsley leaves, for garnish

Place the bacon in a large sauté pan over medium heat. Cook the bacon until brown and crisp, 5–7 minutes. Using a slotted spoon, transfer the bacon to a plate lined with paper towels and set aside. Toss the hot dog slices into the pan and cook until browned on all sides, 3–5 minutes. Transfer the hot dogs to a separate plate and set aside.

Pour out all but 1 tablespoon of the bacon fat from the pan, and then add the ground beef along with the salt and pepper. Using a wooden spoon, break up the ground beef and stir until the beef begins to brown, about 5 minutes. Increase the heat to medium high, and then stir in the onion, bell pepper, garlic, and dried red pepper flakes. Continue cooking until the onion begins to soften and turns translucent, 5–7 minutes. Add the tomato paste and stir to combine, cooking for another 2 minutes.

Pour in the wine, stirring to scrape up any browned bits from the bottom of the pan. Continue cooking until the wine reduces by half, 3–5 minutes. Stir in the banana ketchup, crushed tomatoes, fish sauce, oregano and brown sugar. Bring to a boil, and then cover the pan and simmer over low heat for 20 minutes, stirring often.

During the last 10–15 minutes of cooking the sauce, place the spaghetti in boiling water and cook according to the package instructions. Before draining the spaghetti, reserve 1 cup of the pasta water.

If the spaghetti sauce seems too thick, it can be thinned out with some of the reserved pasta water. Taste the spaghetti sauce and adjust the seasoning with more salt and pepper, and if a sweeter sauce is desired, add more brown sugar.

Divide the spaghetti into individual portions, and then spoon the spaghetti sauce over each portion. Garnish with the reserved hot dogs, bacon bits and parsley.

SALMON AND MISO SOUR SOUP

With a split salmon head, or two, peeking up from a savory *miso* broth, *sinigang* with salmon and *miso* is perhaps one of the most popular variants of the Filipino sour soup. My version is a simple, yet delicious, rendition that features cubed salmon fillet in place of the heads. In addition to the hallmark sour notes provided by the tomatoes and citrus juice, white wine adds another layer of flavor and acidity to the soup as well. *Miso* can be found refrigerated in Asian markets and large supermarkets. It's important to not boil *miso*, as high heat diminishes its flavor—add it at the end. If you have a hankering for fish heads, then by all means, throw a salmon head into the pot and simmer away.

Serves 4–6
Prep Time: 10 minutes
Cooking Time: 35 minutes

2 tablespoons oil
1 small onion, chopped
4 cloves garlic, minced
2 small tomatoes, chopped
1 cup (250 ml) dry white wine
4 cups (1 liter) water
2 tablespoons fish sauce
¼ cup (65 ml) fresh *calamansi* juice, or
    fresh lemon juice, plus more, to taste
½ lb (250 g) *daikon* radish, peeled,
    halved lengthwise and cut into
    ¼-in (6-mm) half-moon slices
2 tablespoons yellow or white *miso*,
    plus more, to taste
1 lb (500 g) skinless, boneless salmon
    fillet (preferably from the belly),
    cut into 1-in (2.5-cm) cubes
Freshly ground black pepper
1 cup (about 50 g) chopped Asian
    mustard greens, or *bok choy*

Heat the oil in a large pot or Dutch oven over moderately high heat. Add the onion and garlic and cook until the onion is tender and translucent, 3–5 minutes. Add the tomatoes to the pot and cook until the tomatoes soften and release some of their liquid, 2–3 minutes. Pour in the white wine, stirring to scrape up any browned bits from the bottom of the pot. Increase the heat to high, and boil the wine until reduced by half, 3–5 minutes.

Stir in the water, fish sauce, *calamansi* juice (or lemon juice, if using), and *daikon*. Bring everything to a boil, and then cover and simmer over low heat until the *daikon* is tender, 10–15 minutes.

Ladle about a ½ cup (125 ml) of the liquid from the pot and into a small bowl. Add the *miso* to the bowl and whisk until the *miso* is completely dissolved. Pour the *miso* mixture into the pot and stir to combine.

Season the salmon with the black pepper, and then add the salmon and the mustard greens (or *bok choy*, if using) to the pot and gently simmer until the salmon is just cooked through and the greens are wilted, 2–3 minutes. Remove the pot from the heat.

Taste the soup and add more *calamansi* juice (or lemon juice, if using) if more sourness is desired, or add more *miso* if a more savory flavor is desired.

Serve immediately with steamed white rice on the side.

MUSSEL, GINGER AND LEMONGRASS SOUP TINOLANG TAHONG

Although a classic Filipino *tinola* is usually prepared with chicken, mussels are a common variant in different parts of the Philippines. One hallmark of *tinola*, whether made with fowl or shellfish, is the use of the fresh leaves from a chili pepper plant, or the fresh leaves from the horseradish tree (*malunggay*). Both leaves can be found frozen at Asian markets, but I prefer to use fresh baby spinach as a more vibrant alternative to the frozen leaves.

With the mussels providing a fresh flavor of the sea, and with ginger and lemongrass lending spice and fragrance, this is a briny and robust soup that can be made without much fuss as part of a quick weeknight meal.

Serves 4–6
Prep Time: 15 minutes
Cooking Time: 45 minutes

2 lbs (1 kg) fresh mussels, in the shell
2 tablespoons oil
1 onion, chopped
One 2-in (5-cm) piece fresh ginger, peeled and minced
1 stalk lemongrass, bottom 4–6 in (10–15 cm) trimmed and finely minced
4 cloves garlic, minced
1 cup (250 ml) dry white wine
¼ cup (65 ml) fish sauce
6 cups (1.5 liters) water
2 small *chayote* squash, peeled, deseeded, and cut into ½-in (1.25-cm) chunks
2 cups (225 g) baby spinach

Rinse and scrub the mussels under cold running water. Remove any fibers or "beards" from the mussels. Discard any mussels with cracked shells, and any mussels that do not close when tapped gently. Set the cleaned mussels aside in the refrigerator.

Heat the oil in a large pot or Dutch oven over medium high heat. Add the onion and cook until tender and translucent, 5–7 minutes. Add the ginger, lemongrass, and garlic to the pot and cook until very fragrant and the garlic begins to brown, 2–3 minutes. Pour in the white wine, stirring to scrape up any browned bits from the bottom of the pot. Increase the heat to high, and boil the wine until reduced by half, 2–3 minutes.

Add the fish sauce and water and stir in the squash. Bring everything to a boil, and then cover and simmer over low heat until the squash is tender, 10–15 minutes. Add the mussels to the pot and close the lid. Continue simmering until all of the mussels have opened, 3–5 minutes. Discard any unopened mussels.

Remove the pot from the heat and stir in the baby spinach—the spinach will wilt from the heat of the soup. Serve the soup with steamed white rice on the side.

COOK'S NOTE: If fresh mussels are not available, you can substitute frozen mussels.

FILIPINO CHICKEN NOODLE SOUP PANCIT SOTANGHON

4 oz (100 g) dried mung bean thread noodles
2 tablespoons Annatto Oil (page 26), or regular vegetable oil, divided
1 lb (500 g) boneless, skinless chicken thighs
Salt, to taste
Freshly ground black pepper, to taste
1 large onion, diced
4 cloves garlic, minced
½ lb (250 g) cherry tomatoes, cut in half
4 cups (1 liter) homemade Chicken Stock (page 21), or store bought chicken stock
2 tablespoons fish sauce, plus more, to taste
1 bitter melon (8–10 in/20–25 cm long), sliced into ¼-in (6-mm) half moons (see How to Prepare Bitter Melon, page 45), or 2 small *chayote* squash, peeled, deseeded and cut into ½-in (1.5-cm) chunks.

Not all chicken soups are created equal. *Pancit sotanghon* is a slurp-worthy chicken noodle soup full of long, translucent mung bean noodles simmered in chicken stock and swimming with bits of tender chicken thigh, cherry tomatoes, and bitter melon. To make things a bit easier to eat, you can choose to pre-cut the dried noodles before cooking, but that would be considered bad luck since long noodles signify long life—which makes this chicken noodle soup not only healthy, but lucky as well. And besides, long noodles are better for slurping.

Serves 4–6 as part of a multi-course meal
Prep Time: 15 minutes
Cooking Time: 45 minutes

Place the dried noodles in a large bowl and cover the noodles with very hot tap water. Set the noodles aside to soften for at least 15 minutes.

Heat 1 tablespoon of the oil in a large pot or Dutch oven over medium high heat. Season the chicken thighs with the salt and pepper, and then place the chicken into the hot oil. Cook the chicken until seared and golden brown on all sides, 3–5 minutes per side. Transfer the chicken to a plate and set aside to cool.

Add the remaining 1 tablespoon of oil to the pot, and then add the onion and cook until tender and translucent, 3–5 minutes. Add the garlic and tomatoes and cook until the tomatoes wilt and release some of their juices, 2–3 minutes. Pour in the Chicken Stock and fish sauce, stirring to scrape up any browned bits from the bottom of the pot.

Chop the browned chicken thighs into small, bite-sized pieces. Add the chicken and the bitter melon (or *chayote* squash, if using) to the pot, increase the heat to high and bring to a boil. Cover the pot, reduce the heat to medium low, and simmer until the vegetables are soft and tender, 10–15 minutes.

Drain the noodles into a fine-mesh sieve and rinse the noodles under warm running water. Add the drained noodles to the soup and continue simmering for 5 more minutes, or until the noodles are completely soft. Taste the soup and adjust the seasoning with more salt and pepper, and additional fish sauce if desired. Serve immediately.

CHAPTER 4

THE ART OF ADOBO

In the context of the Philippines, the term "*adobo*" refers to the Filipino method by which any meat, seafood, fruit, or vegetable is braised in a mixture containing vinegar, bay leaves, garlic, black pepper, and salt. The results of this method are always piquant and robust, yet simultaneously nuanced and well balanced. Apart from these guidelines, any number of additions and variations can be made depending on the recipe's region of origination. For instance, *adobo*s can be made saucy or dry, spicy, or mild. An assortment of spices, seasonings, and flavors can also be added in the form of chili pepper, onion, ginger, lemongrass, and coconut milk, just to name a few. And although the earliest *adobo*s were seasoned with sea salt, soy sauce in *adobo* became commonplace after large numbers of Chinese settled in the Philippines in the sixteenth century. Various *adobo*s are also tinged orange with annatto seeds from Mexico. And while native Filipino vinegars are most commonly called for in *adobo* recipes, Del Monte and Heinz apple cider vinegars gained in popularity following the American occupation of the Philippines.

Hopefully, with the nine different *adobo* recipes I provide in this section, you'll be able to experience just how differently nuanced each dish can be despite being made using a single cooking method. Use these recipes as a baseline, and then create your own variations according to your tastes. And remember, *adobo*s are like snowflakes—no two are the same.

HELPFUL TIPS FOR PREPARING ADOBO

Just about every Filipino has his or her own tips and tricks to making a "perfect" adobo. Here's another tip: there is no perfect adobo! Instead of striving for perfection, strive for something that tastes good to you and that you'd be happy serving your friends and family (unless, of course, they think they have their own perfect version). With that said, here are a few of my own tips and tricks for a flavorful adobo (take them with a grain of salt, or a splash of soy sauce if that's how you roll):

❊ Adobo must always contain some combination of vinegar, bay leaves, garlic, black pepper, and salt or soy sauce.

❊ Although adobo is delicious in all of its tasty forms, be it made from poultry, seafood, or even vegetables, I find that adobo made from pork belly is the most luxurious—there isn't another cut of pork that melds skin, fat, and meat as perfectly and deliciously as does the underside of a pig.

❊ When making adobo, always taste the sauce (if there is one) before serving. Adjust the salt and pepper accordingly, and dilute overpowering vinegar with water, or balance with a touch of sugar, only if necessary.

❊ If adding sugar to an adobo, use a light hand. Sugar should be used only to balance the flavors of adobo, rather than to make it sweet. I realize purists frown upon adding sugar to an adobo, but all three of my grandmas (page 9) add sugar to theirs—and they're the "purist" chicks I know.

❊ The longer an adobo cooks, the less acrid and more pleasant the vinegar becomes.

❊ Because of the vinegar content in adobo, always cook adobo in nonreactive cookware. I usually use stainless steel or enameled cast iron.

❊ Like all braises, adobo is better the next day after the flavors have melded and the meats and vegetables have absorbed these flavors.

❊ When eating someone else's adobo, judge it on the merits of its flavor (does it taste good?), not on whether or not it meets your preconceived notions (does it taste like my mom's adobo?). Different doesn't necessarily mean bad.

SLOW-BRAISED PORK BELLY AND PINEAPPLE ADOBO

A few years ago, during a particularly stifling summer visit to the Philippines, one of my cousins prepared a wonderfully tangy and fruity adobo stew of braised pork and freshly picked pineapples. At the time, I'd never encountered fruit in an adobo. But after experiencing my first bite of this dish, it made complete sense to me—the tartness and sweetness of the pineapples provides a nice balance to the fatty pork.

You can use pork belly with or without the skin for this recipe, though skin-on pork belly will create a richer sauce. And while my cousin prepared her inspirational adobo all those years ago with fresh pineapples from the family farm, canned pineapple chunks, drained, work just as well in this dish.

This adobo is incredibly simple to prepare, but it's definitely a make-ahead dish, so plan accordingly. A long braise makes for an incredibly tender pork belly, and then an overnight stay in the refrigerator allows the cooked pork belly to firm up so that it can be easily cut into neat slices. Chilling the braise in the refrigerator also allows the rendered pork fat to solidify so that it can be easily removed from the cooking liquid and used to sauté the pineapples. You've never had pineapples until you've had pineapples sizzled in pork fat.

Serves 4–6
Prep Time: 5 minutes, plus overnight to mature
Cooking Time: 4 hours

1 tablespoon coarse sea salt, or kosher salt
1 teaspoon coarsely ground black pepper
3 bay leaves
8–10 cloves garlic, smashed with the side of a knife and peeled
¾ cup (185 ml) dark Filipino cane vinegar (*sukang iloco*), or apple cider vinegar
2½ lbs (1.25 kg) slab pork belly
Water, to cover
1 fresh ripe pineapple (2–3 lbs, 1–1.5 kg), peeled, cored and cut into 1-in (2.5-cm) chunks

Combine the salt, black pepper, bay leaves, garlic, and vinegar in a large nonreactive pot or enameled Dutch oven. Nestle the pork belly into the pot, skin side down, and then pour in enough water so that the liquid comes halfway up the pork belly. Bring the pot to a boil over high heat, and then cover and gently simmer over very low heat for at least 3 hours, turning the pork belly over once midway through simmering.

Remove the pot from the heat and allow everything to cool to room temperature. Once cool, place the pot in the refrigerator overnight.

Remove the pork from the refrigerator and uncover. Carefully remove and reserve any congealed fat from atop the cooking liquid. Using tongs, remove the pork from the cooking liquid and place it on a cutting board. Cut the pork into slices that are about ½-in (1.25-cm) thick by 1-in (2.5-cm) wide and set it aside.

Bring the liquid in the pot to a boil over high heat. Continue boiling until the liquid reduces to about 1 cup (250 ml) and thickens slightly—depending on how much water was used, reduction may take anywhere from 10 to 20 minutes. Remove the sauce from the heat and discard the bay leaves.

While the sauce is reducing, heat 1 tablespoon of the reserved pork fat in a large nonstick skillet over medium heat. If you were unable to reserve much pork fat, you can use vegetable oil instead. Working in batches, gently cook the slices of pork belly until lightly browned and jiggly, 1–2 minutes per side, and then transfer the pork belly slices to a large serving platter.

If the pan is dry after cooking the pork belly slices, add another tablespoon of reserved pork fat, or vegetable oil, and heat over medium heat. Working in batches, sauté the pineapple chunks until golden brown, 2–3 minutes per side, and then transfer the pineapple to the platter with the pork belly. Pour the adobo sauce over the pork belly and pineapples and serve with steamed white rice.

COOK'S NOTE: Instead of browning the pork belly and pineapples in a pan, you can cut them into larger chunks and finish them on a hot grill, just until the pork and pineapples are nicely charred with grill marks. Alternatively, you can brown the pork and pineapples on a foil-lined baking sheet placed under the broiler.

AWARD-WINNING FLAVOR

I fell head over heels for this dish after first enjoying it in the Philippines. I loved it so much that, a few years later, I went on to serve a version of it on The Manila Machine, my gourmet Filipino food truck. As it turns out, I wasn't the only one who loved this dish—my Slow-Braised Pork Belly and Pineapple Adobo claimed the Runner-up award for "Best Nouveau Street Food" at the 2010 LA Street Food Fest as judged by a panel of professional chefs and food writers. Yes, this *adobo* is *that* good.

ADOBO ROAST PORK TENDERLOIN

This is an incredibly simple recipe that can be made for a weeknight dinner. Because pork tenderloin is so lean, a long braising time, per the usual *adobo* method, isn't needed. But because of its flavorful marinade, the roasting pork will fill your kitchen with the familiar and enticing *adobo* aromas of vinegar and garlic. And because apples go so well with pork, boiling the reserved marinade with some sweet apple cider makes for a quick and easy pan sauce. Take note that pork loin is much larger than pork tenderloin, and therefore takes much longer to cook. So pay close attention to the packaging label when purchasing the pork tenderloin for this recipe.

Serves 4–6 as part of a multi-course meal
Prep Time: 5 minutes, plus 30 minutes to marinate the pork
Cooking Time: 45 minutes

1 tablespoon minced garlic
1 tablespoon minced shallot
⅔ (160 ml) cup apple cider vinegar
⅓ cup (80 ml) soy sauce
2 bay leaves
1 teaspoon freshly ground black pepper
2 pork tenderloins, about 2½ lbs (1.25 kg) total
½ cup (125 ml) apple cider

Combine the garlic, shallot, vinegar, soy sauce, bay leaves, and black pepper in a small bowl. Place the pork into a shallow baking dish, or a large resealable food storage bag, and pour the marinade over the tenderloins. Cover and marinate the pork in the refrigerator for at least 30 minutes, or overnight if time allows, turning the pork once to ensure even marination.

Preheat the oven to 425°F (220°C).

Remove the pork from the marinade and reserve the marinade. Nestle the pork into a large ovenproof, nonreactive sauté pan, or a small, nonreactive roasting pan, and place the pork in the oven. Roast the pork until it is no longer pink in the middle, or until it reaches an internal temperature of 145°F (63°C) on an instant-read thermometer, 20–25 minutes. Because pork tenderloin is so lean, it dries out easily if roasted for too long, so be watchful. Transfer the pork to a cutting board, and then loosely cover with foil and rest the pork for 10 minutes.

Taking care to not burn yourself on the handles, place the pan over high heat on the stovetop. Pour the apple cider into the pan, stirring to scrape up any browned bits from the bottom of the pan. Add the reserved marinade to the pan and bring to a boil. The liquid must come to a boil in order to rid any bacteria from the pork marinade. Continue to boil and stir until the liquid is reduced to about 1 cup (250 ml), 5–7 minutes.

Cut the pork into ¼-in (6-mm) slices and drizzle with the pan sauce. Serve with steamed white rice.

> **COOK'S NOTE:** This recipe works great on the grill too. Just grill the tenderloins over moderately high heat until grill marks appear on all sides, and then transfer the pork to a cooler part of the grill to finish cooking, 15–20 minutes total. Boil and reduce the marinade as directed above, and drizzle over the grilled tenderloins.

PORK RIBS ADOBO

My two brothers and I once arrived at my grandmother's house late one morning, expecting to eat lunch later that afternoon. Trouble was, my grandma wasn't expecting our company until the next week! Despite this breakdown in communication, my grandma calmly walked into her kitchen and created an amazing *adobo* from what she had on hand: pork ribs, garlic, vinegar, soy sauce, black pepper, and her secret ingredients—pineapple juice and brown sugar.

In no time at all, my brothers and I were feasting like kings, and fighting over the last few tender ribs.

The recipe below is a variation of what my grandmother served us that day, and many other days since. It reminds me of how she can make something fantastic appear from seemingly nothing. And now you can too. Although simple to prepare, the complexities of a great *adobo* (a balance of salty and sour) are achieved with the few ingredients listed.

Serves 4–6 as part of a multi-course meal
Prep Time: 10 minutes
Cooking Time: 2 hours

2–3 lbs (1–1.5 kg) pork baby back ribs, cut into individual ribs
4–5 cloves garlic, minced
¾ cup (185 ml) cider vinegar
¼ cup (65 ml) soy sauce
¼ cup (65 ml) fresh or canned pineapple juice
1 teaspoon coarsely ground black pepper
2 bay leaves
1 tablespoon brown sugar

Lay the ribs into the bottom of a large pot or Dutch oven—it's okay if some of the ribs overlap each other. Add the garlic, vinegar, soy sauce, pineapple juice, and black pepper to the pot and then tuck the bay leaves into the liquid.

Bring the pot to a boil over high heat, and then cover the pot and reduce the heat to low. Simmer the ribs until they are tender, 1 hour 30 minutes to 2 hours. While the ribs are simmering, be sure to toss them in the braising liquid and rearrange them every now and then to ensure even cooking.

Transfer the ribs to a large platter and set aside. Add the brown sugar to the pot and stir to combine. Increase the heat to high and boil until the liquid reduces and thickens slightly, about 5 minutes. Remove the pot from the heat and return the ribs, along with any accumulated juices from the platter, back to the pot. Toss the ribs in the glaze until well coated. Serve with rice.

COOK'S NOTE: According to my grandma, the pineapple juice and brown sugar in this recipe are meant to balance the acidity of the vinegar—not to add unnecessary sweetness.

CHICKEN ADOBO POT PIES

This recipe has all the hallmarks of a great classic chicken pot pie—tender chicken, fresh vegetables, a rich and creamy gravy, and a flaky crust. But with a vinegary *adobo* tang mellowed by creamy coconut milk, these Filipino pot pies are unlike any you've ever had before. To save time, you can use store bought puff pastry instead of making your own crust, and you can also pick the meat off of a store-bought cooked rotisserie chicken rather than browning chicken thighs.

Makes 6 individual pot pies
Prep Time: 15 minutes
Cooking Time: 1 hour, 45 minutes

2 tablespoons oil
1½ lbs (750 g) boneless, skinless chicken
    thighs (about 3–4 thighs)
1 small red onion, diced
1 small red bell pepper, diced
4–5 cloves garlic, minced
2 tablespoons all-purpose flour
½ cup (125 ml) Filipino coconut vinegar,
    or distilled white vinegar
½ cup (125 ml) soy sauce

2 bay leaves
1 teaspoon freshly ground black pepper
1 lb (500 g) russet potatoes, cut into
    small ¼-in (6-mm) cubes
1 cup (250 ml) unsweetened coconut milk
Six 1-cup (250-ml) oven-safe ramekins
1 recipe Flaky Pastry Pie Crust (page 23),
    or store-bought puff pastry
1 large egg, beaten

Preheat the oven to 400°F (200°C).

Heat the oil in a large skillet over moderately-high heat. Add the chicken thighs and cook until just browned on both sides, 4–5 minutes per side. Transfer the chicken to a large plate and set aside to cool.

Add the onion, bell pepper and garlic to the skillet and cook until the onion becomes soft and tender, 4–5 minutes. Sprinkle in the flour and stir to combine, cooking for 2 minutes more. Pour in the vinegar and soy sauce, stirring to scrape up any browned bits from the bottom of the pan, and simmer until the liquid thickens, 2–3 minutes. Reduce the heat to low, and then add the bay leaves, black pepper and potatoes and cover the skillet.

Roughly cut the browned chicken thighs into small cubes, and then stir the cut chicken into the skillet. Add the coconut milk and stir well to combine. Increase the heat to high and bring everything to a boil, stirring frequently. Reduce the heat to low and simmer, uncovered, until the potatoes are tender, about 15 minutes. Remove from the heat, discard the bay leaves, and set aside.

Meanwhile, roll out the prepared Flaky Pastry Pie Crust dough (or store-bought puff pastry, if using) on a lightly floured surface until the dough is about ⅛-in (3-mm) thick. Using one of the ramekins as a template, cut out 6 discs of dough with a paring knife—the discs should be slightly larger than the top of the ramekin. You may have to gather up the scraps of dough and roll it out again in order to get the sixth disc.

Divide the filling among the 6 ramekins. Using a pastry brush, brush the rim of the ramekins with the beaten egg, and then lay a disc of dough on top of each of the ramekins. Using a fork, firmly press and crimp the edges of the dough onto the rim of the ramekins, and then brush the tops of the dough with the rest of the egg. Using a paring knife, cut two to three 1-in (2.5-cm) vents in the top of each pie.

Arrange the pies on a sheet pan and bake in the oven until the crusts are golden brown, 20–30 minutes. Remove from the oven and allow to cool for 5–10 minutes before serving.

BACON AND MUSHROOM ADOBO

Meaty *crimini* mushrooms and smoky bacon are a perfect pair in this simple, yet satisfying, *adobo*. And because mushrooms act as sponges when they are sautéed, they will eagerly absorb much of the bacon fat and *adobo* flavor in which they are cooked—making each bite of this dish a smoky and tangy treat.

Serves 4 as part of a multi-course meal
Prep Time: 20 minutes
Cooking Time: 30 minutes

½ lb (250 g) bacon, finely chopped
2 tablespoons minced shallot
1 tablespoon minced garlic
¼ teaspoon dried red pepper flakes (optional)
1 lb (500 g) *crimini* mushrooms, or white button mushrooms,
  cleaned and cut into fourths lengthwise
¼ cup (65 ml) Filipino cane vinegar, or unseasoned
  rice wine vinegar
2 tablespoons soy sauce
½ teaspoon coarsely ground black pepper
2 bay leaves

Place the bacon in a large sauté pan over medium heat. Cook the bacon until brown and crisp, 5–7 minutes. Using a slotted spoon, transfer the bacon to a plate lined with a paper towel. Set the bacon aside.

Add the shallot, garlic and red pepper flakes (if using) to the pan and cook until the shallot softens and the garlic just begins to brown, 2–3 minutes. Add the mushrooms to the pan and stir until the mushrooms absorb most of the fat in the pan, about 1 minute.

Pour in the vinegar and soy sauce, stirring to scrape up any browned bits from the bottom of the pan. Increase the heat to high and bring to a boil. Stir in the black pepper and drop in the bay leaves. Reduce the heat to low and simmer, uncovered, until the mushrooms shrink in size and become tender, 10–15 minutes. Stir in the reserved bacon bits and serve over steamed white rice.

VEGETARIAN BELL PEPPER ADOBO ADOBONG SILI

My grandfather used to grow an incredible bounty of vegetables in his Delano, California backyard. He harvested everything from eggplant, to squash, to bitter melon. Though he didn't have a huge plot of land, he was always able to grow more than enough vegetables for the family, enabling him to happily share his yield with neighbors and friends. Among my grandfather's crops, my favorite might have been the mild, finger-length green chili peppers that he once grew. I wasn't quite so enamored with the chili peppers themselves, as much as I was in love with how my grandmother would prepare these chili peppers. She would take the freshly picked peppers and simply simmer them in soy and vinegar. Because the chili peppers were so mild, they made for a great vegetarian *adobo*, imparting a wonderfully fruity and peppery aroma and flavor—without much spice or heat. I never figured out the exact type of chili pepper that my grandfather grew, and I never see them in any stores—perhaps because my grandfather smuggled the seeds in from the Philippines once upon a time. Nevertheless, my updated version made with colorful bell peppers is a close facsimile, and a comforting reminder, of that *adobo* once made from my grandfather's chili peppers.

Serves 4–6
Prep Time: 15 minutes
Cooking Time: 30 minutes

2 tablespoons oil
1 red onion, thinly sliced
5–6 cloves garlic, smashed with the side of a knife and peeled
4 bell peppers of differing colors (green, red, yellow, orange), deseeded and cut into thin strips
¼ cup (65 ml) Filipino coconut vinegar, or distilled white vinegar
¼ cup (65 ml) soy sauce
¼ cup (65 ml) water
1 tablespoon brown sugar
1 teaspoon freshly ground black pepper
1 bay leaf

Heat the oil in a large sauté pan over moderately high heat. Add the onion and garlic and sauté until the onion is soft and translucent, 3–5 minutes. Toss in the bell peppers and sauté until they just begin to soften, 3–5 minutes.

Pour in the vinegar, soy sauce and water, stirring to scrape up any browned bits from the bottom of the pan. Stir in the brown sugar and black pepper, and add the bay leaf. Increase the heat to high and bring the liquid to a boil. Reduce the heat to low, and simmer uncovered for 20 minutes, or until the bell peppers become tender but not mushy. Discard the bay leaf and serve the *adobo* with steamed white rice.

ADOBO: WHAT'S IN A NAME?

Despite foreign influence on Filipino cuisine, Filipino *adobo* is indigenous and unique to the Philippines, existing before colonial rule. In the Philippines, "*adobo*" refers to a technique, rather than a singular dish. In the Spanish context, *adobo* generally refers to a marinade used to flavor meats, whereas Mexican *adobo* refers to any number of spices. In all likelihood, Spanish colonists simply applied their term to what the Filipinos were already cooking and eating because it was similar in appearance to Spanish *adobo*, though not prepared the same way.

SQUID ADOBO ADOBONG PUSIT

This is another variation on *adobo* that showcases just how simply the dish can be prepared—just simmer squid until it is yielding and tender for a rich seafood *adobo*.

You can use pre-cleaned frozen squid tubes and tentacles found in the freezer section in Asian markets and most grocery stores. But I prefer to use whole medium-sized squid (the tube is about 4 in/10 cm in length) so that I can use their ink in the *adobo* sauce. Not only does the ink provide a wonderful flavor, but it also gives the dish a deeper color. It is purely optional, but to harvest the ink from whole squid, pierce the ink sacs found in the body near the eyes and drain the ink into a small bowl.

Because squid tend to shrink from long simmering, I prefer to leave the squid tubes whole, but you may cut them into thick rings if you'd like.

Serves 4–6 as part of a multi-course meal
Prep Time: 15 minutes
Cooking Time: 1 hour

1 tablespoon oil
1 small onion, thinly sliced
½ teaspoon coarse salt
6 cloves garlic, minced
½ cup (125 ml) dark Filipino cane vinegar (*sukang iloco*), or apple cider vinegar
⅓ cup (80 ml) soy sauce
2 bay leaves
1 teaspoon coarsely ground black pepper
2 lbs (1 kg) cleaned squid tubes and tentacles (fresh, or previously frozen)
Squid ink (optional)

Heat the oil in a large sauté pan over moderately-high heat. Add the onion and salt and sauté until the onion is soft and translucent, 3–5 minutes. Add the garlic and cook until just beginning to brown, 2–3 minutes.

Pour in the vinegar and soy sauce, stirring to scrape up any browned bits from the bottom of the pan. Tuck the bay leaves into the liquid, and then stir in the black pepper, squid and ink (if using).

Bring the liquid to a boil, and then reduce the heat to low. As the squid cook, they will shrink and release some liquid. Gently simmer the squid, stirring occasionally, until very tender, about 45 minutes.

Discard the bay leaves and serve the *adobo* with steamed white rice.

CLASSIC CHICKEN ADOBO

This is the chicken *adobo* I grew up with—everything is thrown into a pot and simmered, the sauce is boiled and reduced, done. It is *adobo* in its simplest, most basic, and perhaps best form.

But don't confuse basic with bland. As the sauce for this dish finishes and boils, the bubbling helps to emulsify the liquid with the chicken fat in the pan, creating a simple yet flavorful glaze. And even though the chicken isn't browned or seared, it still achieves a beautiful brown sheen from the luscious sauce.

Serves 4–6 as part of a multi-course meal
Prep Time: 5 minutes
Cooking Time: 45 minutes

¼ cup (65 ml) soy sauce
½ cup (125 ml) white Filipino cane vinegar, or distilled white vinegar
6–8 cloves garlic, smashed with the side of a knife and peeled
1 teaspoon whole black peppercorns
2 bay leaves
6 skin-on, bone-in chicken thighs

Place the soy sauce, vinegar, garlic, black peppercorns, and bay leaves in a large, nonreactive sauté pan, and then nestle the chicken thighs, skin side down, into the pan. Bring the liquid to a boil over high heat, and then cover and simmer over low heat for 20 minutes. Turn the chicken over, and then cover and simmer for another 10 minutes.

Uncover the pan, and then increase the heat to high and return the sauce to a boil. While occasionally turning and basting the chicken, continue boiling the sauce, uncovered, until it is reduced by half and thickens slightly, 5–7 minutes. Serve with steamed white rice.

VARIATIONS: While the sauce is reducing, transfer the chicken thighs, skin side up, to a foil-lined sheet pan. Brown the chicken thighs underneath the broiler for 3–5 minutes.

Use freshly ground black pepper instead of whole peppercorns.

For a "drier" chicken *adobo*, you can reduce the sauce until it is almost completely evaporated. The chicken will then begin to fry in its own fat that is still left in the pan. This is how my grandmother finishes her *adobo*.

For a saucier *adobo*, double the amount of soy sauce and vinegar.

To make this *adobo* as an appetizer, use 2 lbs (1 kg) of chicken wings instead of thighs.

RED WINE AND SHORT RIBS ADOBO

Short ribs are perhaps the best cut of beef for use in long-simmered stews and braises. When braising short ribs, it's best to simmer them for a minimum of two hours—which is why I love using them in an *adobo*. When gently simmered, the bones, meat and fat of the short ribs all combine to lend a more robust flavor to the braising liquid.

In this case, the braising liquid is comprised of red wine, red wine vinegar, and soy sauce. Dry red wine is always great when paired with beef, but it also lends another layer of acidity to the dish as well. And while red wine vinegar isn't usually used in Filipino cooking, it blends seamlessly with the red wine while still providing the vinegar bite needed in an *adobo*.

While the ingredients for this recipe may seem out of place for an *adobo*, they all come together for an intensely flavored stew that is undeniably delicious, and undeniably Filipino.

Serves 4–6
Prep Time: 10 minutes
Cooking Time: 2 hours, 30 minutes

1 tablespoon oil
3 lbs (1.5 kg) bone-in beef short ribs (about 6–8 meaty short ribs)
Coarse salt
1 large onion, diced
8–10 cloves garlic, smashed with the side of a knife and peeled
1 cup (250 ml) dry red wine
½ cup (125 ml) red wine vinegar
½ cup (125 ml) soy sauce
2 bay leaves
1 teaspoon coarsely ground black pepper
Water, to cover

Heat the oil in a large, deep, nonreactive pot over moderately high heat. Season the short ribs on all sides with the salt, and then add the short ribs to the pot in batches. Cook the short ribs until brown and crusty on all sides, 3–5 minutes per side. Transfer the short ribs to a large platter and set aside.

Pour off all but 1 tablespoon of fat from the pot, and then return the pot to medium heat. Add the onion and garlic and sauté until the onion just begins to soften, about 5 minutes. Reduce the heat to low and pour in the red wine, stirring to scrape up any browned bits from the bottom of the pot. Simmer the red wine for 2–3 minutes.

Add the red wine vinegar, soy sauce, bay leaves, and the coarsely ground black pepper to the pot. Return the short ribs, along with any accumulated juices from its platter, to the pot. Add enough water to the pot to just barely cover the short ribs, and then bring to a boil over high heat. Decrease the heat to low, and then cover and simmer for at least 2 hours, turning the ribs occasionally to ensure even cooking. While the ribs are simmering, be sure to skim off and discard any fat that rises to the surface of the cooking liquid. The ribs are done when they are fork-tender and falling off the bone.

Skim any remaining fat that may have risen to the surface of the cooking liquid, and then transfer the short ribs to a large platter and set aside. Increase the heat to high and bring the liquid in the pot to a boil. Continue boiling until the liquid is reduced to about 2 cups—this can take anywhere from 10–30 minutes depending on how much water was previously added. Discard the bay leaves and taste the sauce; adjust the seasoning with more salt and pepper if needed.

Serve the short ribs with steamed white rice, and drizzle some of the sauce over the ribs and rice.

CHAPTER 5

MAIN DISHES

ULAM

The Filipino term "*ulam*" refers to any dish eaten with rice. So by that definition, *adobos* also count as *ulam*. In this section though, I highlight the wide spectrum of various other Filipino cooking techniques and their resultant tasty offerings.

These are the heavy hitters of Filipino cuisine, weighty dishes of meat, poultry and seafood that are filling enough on their own, but are downright feast-worthy when served with rice—as they always are.

From the broiler to the oven to the grill to the stovetop, simmered in coconut milk, sautéed in oil, bathed in tomato sauce, or deep-fried, the dishes in this section will provide you ample opportunities to delight, entertain, and satisfy whoever is lucky enough to sit at your dinner table.

FILIPINO PAN-SEARED STEAK WITH ONIONS BISTEK

Evolved from the Spanish dish, *bistec encebollado* (also steak and onions), Filipino *bistek* features beef marinated in a salty-tangy marinade of soy and citrus juice—simple enough for a quick weeknight dinner.

Serves 4–6
Prep Time: 10 minutes, plus at least 30 minutes to marinate
Cooking Time: 30 minutes

¼ cup (65 ml) soy sauce
¼ cup (65 ml) fresh *calamansi* juice, or fresh lemon juice
2 lbs (1 kg) flank steak
2 tablespoons vegetable oil, divided
1 large onion, cut into thin rings
6 cloves garlic, minced
¼ cup (65 ml) water
2 teaspoons brown sugar
Salt, to taste
Freshly ground black pepper, to taste

Combine the soy sauce and *calamansi* juice (or lemon juice, if using) in a small bowl. Place the steak in a large resealable food storage bag, or in a shallow baking dish, and pour the marinade over the steak. Marinate the steak for at least 30 minutes, or up to 2 hours, in the refrigerator.

Remove the steak from the marinade and reserve the marinade. Pat the steak dry all over with paper towels. If the steak is too big to fit into a large sauté pan, cut the steak in half. Heat 1 tablespoon of the oil in a large sauté pan over moderately high heat. When the oil is hot and shimmering, add the steak to the pan and cook until the steak is seared and nicely browned on both sides, 4–5 minutes per side for medium-rare doneness. If you had to cut your steak in half, cook each half one at a time so that you don't overcrowd your pan. Transfer the seared steak to a cutting board to rest for at least 10 minutes.

Add the remaining 1 tablespoon of oil to the pan and heat over moderately high heat. Toss the onion rings into the pan and cook until the onion softens, 3–5 minutes. Add the garlic to the pan and cook until the garlic just begins to brown, 2–3 minutes. Pour the water and the reserved marinade into the pan, stirring to scrape up any browned bits from the bottom of the pan. Stir in the sugar and bring the sauce to a boil. Cover the pan, and then simmer over low heat for 5 minutes.

Meanwhile, thinly slice the seared steak across the grain. Taste the sauce in the pan and adjust the seasoning with salt and pepper if needed.

Drizzle the sliced steak with the sauce and onion, and serve with steamed white rice.

> **COOK'S NOTE:** For a saucier version of *bistek*, double the amount of soy sauce and *calamansi* juice (or lemon juice, if using). For a thicker sauce, stir 2 teaspoons of cornstarch into the ¼ cup (65 ml) of water in the recipe. Add the cornstarch slurry to the pan along with the reserved marinade, bring to a boil, and then simmer over low heat until the sauce thickens.

FILIPINO MEATLOAF EMBUTIDO

If there's one comfort food that both Americans and Filipinos can identify with, it's meatloaf. Filipino meatloaf, or *embutido*, does have a few distinct and tasty advantages over its American counterpart. *Embutido* is usually made with ground pork rather than beef, and *embutido* is usually fortified with whole hard-boiled eggs stuffed right into the loaf. The hard-boiled eggs not only act as extenders for the meat, but they also make for a beautiful presentation once the meatloaf is sliced. Although traditional *embutido* is usually wrapped in foil and steamed, I prefer to bake *embutido* uncovered so that it can be smothered with a sweet banana ketchup glaze. My rendition of *embutido* also uses 1 lb (500 g) each of ground beef and ground pork, but you can choose to use 2 lbs (1 kg) of all beef or all pork.

Serves 4–6
Prep Time: 20 minutes
Cooking Time: 1 hour, 30 minutes

For the meatloaf:
1/3 cup (20 g) *panko* bread crumbs
1 cup (250 ml) milk
1 tablespoon soy sauce
1 tablespoon fish sauce
2 teaspoons freshly ground black pepper
1 tablespoon Homemade Banana Ketchup (page 24), or store-bought banana ketchup
2 tablespoons oil
1 onion, diced
1 green bell pepper, deseeded and diced
1 red bell pepper, deseeded and diced
1 teaspoon salt
4 cloves garlic, minced (2 teaspoons)
1 lb (500 g) ground beef
1 lb (500 g) ground pork
3 hard-boiled eggs, shells removed

For the glaze:
1/3 cup (80 ml) Homemade Banana Ketchup (page 24), or 1/3 cup (80 ml) store-bought banana ketchup

Preheat the oven to 350°F (175°C).

In a large bowl, combine the bread crumbs, milk, soy sauce, fish sauce, black pepper, and 1 tablespoon of Homemade Banana Ketchup.

Set aside for 5–10 minutes.

Meanwhile, heat the oil in a large wok or skillet over high heat. Add the onion, the green and red bell peppers, and the salt and stir-fry until the onion softens and is translucent, 3–5 minutes. Add the garlic and stir-fry until the garlic just begins to brown, about 2 minutes. Remove from the heat and allow the vegetables to cool in the pan.

Add the ground beef, ground pork, and cooled vegetables to the large bowl with the bread crumb mixture. Using a rubber spatula, or your hands, gently mix until everything is well combined.

Using half of the meat mixture, form a rectangular bed (about 10 x 5 in/25 x 13 cm) in the center of a large foil-lined sheet pan. Nestle the three eggs along the center of the bed. Form a loaf shape around the eggs with the remainder of the meat mixture, making sure that the eggs are completely enclosed. Brush the 1/3 cup of Homemade Banana Ketchup onto all sides of the meatloaf.

Place the meatloaf in the oven for 60–75 minutes, or until an instant-read thermometer (inserted into the meat, not the eggs) registers 145°F (63°C). To further brown and caramelize the glaze, place the meatloaf under the broiler for an additional 5–10 minutes.

Remove the meatloaf from the oven and rest for 10 minutes before slicing. Serve with steamed white rice.

GRILLED LEMONGRASS CHICKEN CHICKEN INASAL

Chicken *inasal* originates from Bacolod City in the Western Visayas region of the Philippines, where grilled chicken is more than just grilled chicken. In Bacolod, grill masters bathe chicken pieces in a marinade of vinegar, citrus juice, lemongrass and salt. The chicken is then skewered and slowly grilled while lovingly brushed with annatto oil. The finished dish is fragrant and moist with smoke and citrus, and tinged a beautiful orange color from the annatto. I prefer to use chicken leg quarters (legs and thighs still connected) for this recipe because they cook evenly and tend to not dry out, but you can use breasts and wings, or even a whole butterflied chicken, with equally great results.

Serves 4–6
***Prep Time: 20 minutes, plus at least
   4 hours to marinate***
Cooking Time: 45 minutes

½ cup (125 ml) fresh *calamansi* juice, or
   fresh lemon juice
¼ cup (65 ml) Filipino coconut vinegar, or
   white distilled vinegar
6 cloves garlic, minced
One 1-in (2.5-cm) piece fresh ginger,
   peeled and minced
2 lemongrass stalks, bottom 4–6 in

(10–15 cm) trimmed and minced
½ teaspoon dried red pepper flakes
3 tablespoons brown sugar
1 tablespoon coarse salt
6 skin-on, bone-in chicken leg quarters
   (legs and thighs still connected)

For the glaze:
¼ cup (65 ml) Annatto Oil (page 26), or
   regular vegetable oil
2 tablespoons Homemade Banana
   Ketchup (page 24), or store-bought
   banana ketchup

Combine the *calamansi* juice, vinegar, garlic, ginger, lemongrass, dried red pepper flakes, brown sugar and salt in a large bowl. Whisk until the sugar and salt dissolve completely.

Place the chicken in a large shallow baking dish. Pour the marinade over the chicken and cover. Marinate the chicken in the refrigerator for at least 4 hours, or overnight, turning the pieces over once to ensure even marination.

Clean and oil the grates of your grill and preheat for indirect, medium-heat cooking (one hot side, and one cool side of the grill)

Combine the Annatto Oil and Home-made Banana Ketchup in a medium bowl and whisk to combine and form a glaze.

Remove the chicken from the marinade and discard the marinade. Brush some of the glaze all over the chicken.

Place the chicken, skin side down, on the hot side of the grill and brush the back with more glaze. Close the lid and grill for 10 minutes, or until the chicken is nicely browned with grill marks. Flip the chicken and place it on the cool side of the grill. Brush the chicken with more glaze. Close the lid and continue to grill the chicken, while occasionally basting with glaze, until the chicken is completely cooked through and an instant-read thermometer inserted into the thickest part of the thigh reads 160°F (72°C), 20–30 minutes more.

Serve with steamed white rice and Pickled Green Papaya (page 22) on the side.

SHRIMP IN COCONUT MILK GINATAANG HIPON

The term "*ginataan*" refers to a Filipino preparation in which a dish is cooked in coconut milk. While most anything can benefit from this method, my favorite ingredient to simmer in coconut milk is shrimp. The natural sweetness of shrimp is a perfect partner to rich coconut milk.

This recipe calls for the use of shrimp stock, which lends a ton of shrimp flavor to this dish. If you don't have any shrimp stock already made, you can substitute water. In that case, it is best to use head-on, shell-on shrimp because so much flavor can be extracted from the heads and shells. And depending on your preference for spice, the amount of chili peppers can be increased or decreased as needed.

Serves 4–6 as part of a multi-course meal
Prep Time: 10 minutes
Cooking Time: 15 minutes

1 tablespoon high-heat oil
1 small onion, chopped
4 cloves garlic, minced (2 teaspoons)
1-in (2.5-cm) piece fresh ginger, peeled and minced
1–2 Thai chili peppers, split in half lengthwise with stems intact
1½ cups (375 ml) canned unsweetened coconut milk
1 cup (250 ml) Shrimp Stock (page 21)
1 tablespoon fish sauce
1 lb (500 g) fresh of previously frozen, peeled and deveined medium shrimp
1 tablespoon fresh *calamansi* juice, or fresh lime juice
Salt, to taste
Freshly ground black pepper, to taste

Heat a large wok or sauté pan over high heat until a drop of water sizzles and evaporates on contact. Swirl the oil into the pan, and then add the onion and stir-fry until the onion wilts and begins to lightly brown, 2–3 minutes. Add the garlic, ginger, and chili peppers, and stir-fry until fragrant and the garlic just begins to brown, about 1 minute.

Pour in the coconut milk, Shrimp Stock and fish sauce, stirring to scrape up any browned bits from the bottom of the pan. Bring the liquid to a boil, and then reduce the heat to low and simmer until the liquid reduces and thickens slightly, 3-5 minutes.

Stir in the shrimp and *calamansi* juice (or lime juice if using) and continue to simmer until the shrimp are cooked through, 3–5 minutes more. Taste the sauce and season with salt and freshly ground black pepper as needed. Remove from the heat and serve immediately with steamed white rice.

BRAISED OXTAIL WITH ROASTED VEGETABLES IN PEANUT SAUCE KARE KARE

I was never really a fan of *kare kare*, a rustic Filipino stew of oxtails, eggplant, long beans, and peanut sauce—until I started making it for myself. Because *kare kare* is best when served with the salty sautéed shrimp paste (*ginisang bagoong*), the traditional peanut sauce is usually prepared with no spice or seasoning in order to accommodate the salty condiment. Saltiness of the shrimp paste aside, I still didn't think it was reason enough to be satisfied with, dare I say it, such a bland peanut sauce. While traditionalists may bristle at that last sentence, I've found that the addition of cocoa powder, a bit of sugar, and fish sauce, as well as some chili paste and citrus juice, all blend together to create a really well-balanced peanut sauce with deep—but not overpowering—flavors. And despite these additional flavors, there is still plenty of room for the traditional salty condiment *bagoong*—which really makes this whole dish sing. In addition to my peanut sauce tinkering, this recipe also deviates from the traditional *kare kare* in that the oxtails are briefly roasted in the oven to render out some fat. After the oxtails are roasted, the vegetables are tossed in the rendered fat and roasted as well. This extra step provides much more flavor, and is well worth the time and effort.

Serves 4–6
Prep Time: 15 minutes
Cooking Time: 4 hours

3 lbs (1½ kg) beef oxtails
Salt, to taste
Freshly ground black pepper, to taste
1 onion, cut into ½-in (1.25-cm) slices
½ lb (250 g) Asian eggplant (about 2 medium eggplants), halved lengthwise and cut into ½-in (1.25-cm) thick half-moon slices
½ lb (250 g) long beans, trimmed and cut into 2-in (5-cm) pieces
Water, to cover
2 bay leaves
2 teaspoons whole black peppercorns
2 tablespoons Annatto Oil (page 26), or regular vegetable oil
6 cloves garlic, minced
½ cup (250 g) all-natural smooth peanut butter
1 teaspoon unsweetened cocoa powder
2 teaspoons sugar
2 teaspoons fish sauce
1–2 teaspoons *sambal oelek* chili paste (optional)
2 teaspoons fresh *calamansi* juice, or fresh lime juice

Preheat the oven to 400°F (200°C).

Season the oxtails liberally with salt and pepper, and place the oxtails in a large roasting pan. Roast the oxtails in the oven, turning occasionally, until golden brown on all sides, about 30 minutes. Remove the roasting pan from the oven, and then transfer the oxtails to a large pot or Dutch oven and set aside. Don't turn off the oven or wash out the roasting pan, as you will still need them to roast the vegetables.

Place the onion, eggplant, and long beans in the roasting pan and toss so that the vegetables are coated in the fat left from the oxtails. If there isn't enough fat to coat all the vegetables, add a scant tablespoon of canola or vegetable oil. Roast the vegetables in the oven until tender, 10–15 minutes. Remove the roasting pan from the oven and transfer the vegetables to a large plate. Loosely cover the vegetables with foil and set aside. Turn off the oven.

While the vegetables are roasting, pour enough water into the pot of oxtails to cover the oxtails by at least 1 in (2.5 cm). Add the bay leaves and the black peppercorns. Bring the pot to a boil over high heat, and then cover and simmer over low heat until the oxtails are fork-tender, at least 2 hours. While the oxtails are simmering, skim off and discard any foam or fat that rises to the surface of the water.

Transfer the oxtails to a large platter and set aside. Pour the broth from the pot through a fine mesh strainer set over a large bowl. Discard the bay leaves and black peppercorns and set the broth aside.

Return the same pot to moderately high heat and swirl in the Annatto Oil. Add the garlic and cook until the garlic just begins to brown, 1–2 minutes. Pour 3 cups (750 ml) of the reserved broth into the pot, stirring to scrape up any browned bits from the bottom of the pot. The remaining broth in the bowl can be reserved and frozen for another use.

Stir the peanut butter into the pot and whisk until thoroughly combined. Add the cocoa powder, sugar, fish sauce, chili paste (if using) and *calamansi* juice (or lime juice), and stir to combine. Increase the heat to high, and then boil and reduce the sauce until slightly thickened, 5–10 minutes.

You can optionally now pick the meat from the oxtail and discard the bones, or you can serve the oxtails whole. Stir the meat, or whole oxtail, back into the pot, along with the roasted vegetables, and simmer until the vegetables are just warmed through, 2–3 minutes. Taste the sauce and adjust the seasonings as needed. Keep in mind, when serving the *kare kare* with shrimp paste—a very salty condiment—less salt will be needed in the sauce.

Serve with rice and plenty of Sautéed Shrimp Paste (page 26) on the side.

> **COOK'S NOTE:** The reserved beef broth from this recipe can be used in addition to water in the Beef Short Rib Sour Soup recipe (page 62), or in the Spicy Beef Stew recipe (page 88).

SPICY BEEF STEW CALDERETA

Like most beef stews, *caldereta* features chunks of beef slowly simmered in a flavorful broth or sauce. But what sets *caldereta* apart is the addition of liver pâté—often in the form of canned liverwurst spread—that is whisked into the sauce. While liverwurst might seem like a strange ingredient for a beef stew, it imparts a deeply rich flavor while also helping to thicken the spicy tomato-based sauce.

Serves 4–6
Prep Time: 25 minutes
Cooking Time: 2 hours, 30 minutes

2 lbs (1 kg) beef chuck, cut into 1-in (2.5-cm) cubes
Salt, to taste
Freshly ground black pepper, to taste
2 tablespoons oil
1 onion, diced
1 large carrot, diced
4 cloves garlic, minced
½ teaspoon dried red pepper flakes, plus more, to taste
1 tablespoon tomato paste
1 cup (250 ml) red wine
¼ cup (65 ml) soy sauce
One 4.25 oz (120 g) can prepared liverwurst spread
One 8 oz (250 ml) can tomato sauce
Water, to cover
2 bay leaves
1 red bell pepper, deseeded and diced
1 green bell pepper, deseeded and diced

Season the beef with the salt and black pepper. Heat the oil in a large pot or Dutch oven over moderately high heat. Working in batches, brown the beef on all sides, 5–7 minutes total. Set the browned beef aside on a large platter.

Add the onion, carrot, garlic, and red pepper flakes to the pot and cook until the onion becomes soft and translucent, 3–5 minutes. Stir in the tomato paste and cook until the tomato paste is completely incorporated into the vegetables and begins to brown, 1–2 minutes.

Pour in the red wine and soy sauce, stirring to scrape up any browned bits from the bottom of the pot. Bring the liquid to a boil and continue cooking until reduced by half, about 3 minutes. Add the liverwurst and tomato sauce and stir well to combine.

Return the browned beef, and any accumulated juices from its platter, to the pot. Pour in just enough water to cover the beef and then add the bay leaves. Bring the pot to a boil and then cover and simmer, stirring occasionally, over low heat until the beef is fork-tender, about 2 hours. For the last 10 minutes of cooking, stir in the diced bell peppers.

The *caldereta* can be served with rice, or a crusty baguette.

CRUNCHY PORK BELLY LECHON KAWALI

Lechon kawali is a revered Filipino delicacy of very tender, yet amazingly crisp, deep-fried pork belly. Although it may seem like an easy enough dish, there is more to it than simply tossing a slab of pork into a vat of hot grease. To avoid tough meat, the pork must first be simmered in seasoned water until very tender. After simmering, the pork belly is refrigerated overnight to remove any moisture from the skin—the drier the skin, the crispier it becomes when fried. After simmering and air-drying, the pork belly is finally ready to be fried—*lechon kawali* is worth the wait. Although the recipe in this book calls for the pork belly to be fried only once, a second or even third frying is not out of the question in some parts of the Philippines. In the Ilocos Norte region for example, *lechon kawali* is better known as *bagnet* or Ilocano *chicharón*. Various Ilocano markets and street vendors will fry the prepared pork belly, leave it to drain and rest on paper towels or newspapers, and then fry the pork belly for a second or third time for an even crunchier exterior. While multiple fryings *do* result in crunchier pork, a single fry will still reward you with golden nuggets of tender belly meat, buttery fat and crispy crunchy skin.

Serves 4–6 as part of a multi-course meal
Prep Time: 10 minutes, plus overnight to dehydrate
Cooking Time: 2 hours, 30 minutes

2½ lbs (1.25 kg) skin-on pork belly
6 cloves garlic, smashed with the side of a knife and peeled
3 tablespoons coarse sea salt, or kosher salt
1 tablespoon whole black peppercorns
3 bay leaves
Water, to cover
High-heat cooking oil, for frying

Nestle the pork belly, skin-side down, into a large pot or Dutch oven. Add the garlic, salt, black peppercorns, and bay leaves and pour in enough water to just cover the pork belly. Place the pot over high heat and bring to a boil. Cover the pot, reduce the heat to low, and simmer for at least 2 hours until the pork is very tender.

Transfer the pork, skin-side up, to a cooling rack set over a baking sheet and pat the pork belly dry with paper towels. Place the pork belly, uncovered on the cooling rack, into the refrigerator overnight. You can strain and save the pork broth in the pot for another use, just be aware of the salinity of the broth when using in other recipes.

Remove the pork from the refrigerator and cut into 1-in (2.5-cm) cubes.

In a large wok, or a deep pot, pour enough oil to reach a depth of at least 4 in (10 cm), or enough oil to submerge the cubes of pork belly. Heat the oil over moderately high heat until the oil reaches 375°F (190°C) on a deep fry thermometer. Alternatively, you can insert a dry wooden skewer or chopstick into the hot oil; if bubbles quickly rise to the surface around the stick, the oil is hot enough and ready for frying.

Carefully drop 5–6 cubes of pork into the hot oil, gently flipping and stirring the pork to ensure that the cubes don't stick together. Fry the pork until the meat is golden brown and the skin is blistered and crisp, 3–5 minutes.

Remove the pork from the oil and place it on a plate lined with paper towels. Repeat until all of the pork is fried. The temperature of the oil will drop with each addition of the pork, so be sure to maintain a frying temperature between 350°F (175°C) and 375°F (190°C), and that the pork browns and crisps in 3–5 minutes time.

Serve the fried pork belly with steamed white rice and a side of Tomato Relish with Fish Sauce and Shallots (page 23).

COOK'S NOTES: After frying, you can freeze the pork belly for future use. Just thaw the fried pork belly, and refry again until heated through and crisp.

You can also use *lechon kawali* to make Stewed Vegetables with Pork Belly (page 49).

FRAGRANT AND SWEET BRAISED PORK BELLY
HUMBA

Humba is a dish hailing from the Eastern Visayas region of the Philippines. *Humba* is very similar to an *adobo* in that it uses soy sauce and vinegar as a braising liquid. But what makes *humba* different from an *adobo* is that *humba* is markedly sweeter, and it also includes a bevy of Chinese ingredients such as fermented black beans, cinnamon, and star anise—all of which make for an incredibly piquant and aromatic stew. While a traditional *humba* is tasty enough, I love adding a few cups of coffee to the braising liquid for yet another dimension of flavor. If you aren't a coffee drinker, you can simply substitute with water.

It is traditional, and best, to use skin-on pork belly for this dish—the long braise will render the skin soft and jelly-like while simultaneously enriching the sauce. After braising the pork belly, an overnight stay in the refrigerator allows the cooked pork to absorb more flavors, and it also lets the pork firm up so that it can be easily cut into neat slices. Chilling the braise in the refrigerator also allows the rendered pork fat to solidify so that it can be easily removed from the cooking liquid.

Although this is a make-ahead dish, it is simple to prepare and well worth the time, so plan accordingly.

Serves 4–6
Prep Time: 20 minutes, plus overnight to mature
Cooking Time: 4 hours

One 2½-lb (1.25-kg) slab skin-on pork belly
2 tablespoons high-heat cooking oil, divided
1 onion, diced
6 cloves garlic, minced
One 1-in (2.5-cm) piece fresh ginger, minced
¼ cup (50 g) fermented black beans
¼ cup (65 ml) soy sauce
¼ cup (65 ml) Filipino cane vinegar, or cider vinegar
3 cups (750 ml) strongly brewed coffee
¼ cup (45 g) brown sugar
One 4-in (10-cm) cinnamon stick
1 bay leaf
2 star anise
Water, to cover

Using the tip of a sharp knife, score the skin across the entire pork belly, first making vertical cuts, and then horizontal cuts, that are all about ½-in (1.25-cm) apart. Be sure to make shallow cuts through the skin and to the fat, but not through to the meat. Scoring the skin in this manner will allow much of the fat to render out from the belly. Rub 1 tablespoon of the cooking oil onto the skin side of the pork belly.

Heat the remaining 1 tablespoon of oil in a large nonreactive pot or enameled Dutch oven over moderately high heat, swirling the oil to make sure it covers the entire bottom of the pot. Place the pork belly, skin-side down, into the pot and cook until the skin is golden brown, 5–7 minutes. Flip the pork belly over and sear the other side until golden brown, 5–7 minutes more. Using tongs, transfer the pork belly to a large platter and set aside.

Pour off all but 1 tablespoon of fat from the pot and return the pot to moderately high heat. Add the onion and cook until soft and translucent, 5–7 minutes. Add the garlic, ginger, and black beans, and sauté until the garlic and ginger become fragrant, 1–2 minutes. Add the soy sauce and vinegar, stirring to scrape up any browned bits from the bottom of the pot.

Pour in the coffee, and then stir in the brown sugar to dissolve. Return the pork belly, along with any accumulated juices from its platter, to the pot and add the cinnamon stick, bay leaf, and star anise. If needed, add enough water to just barely cover the pork belly. Bring the pot to a boil over high heat, and then cover and gently simmer over very low heat for at least 2–3 hours, turning the pork belly over once midway through simmering.

Remove the pot from the heat and allow the pork and cooking liquid to cool to room temperature. Once cool, place the pot in the refrigerator overnight.

Remove the pork from the refrigerator and uncover. Carefully remove and discard any congealed fat that rests on top of the cooking liquid. Using tongs, remove the pork belly from the cooking liquid and place the pork on a cutting board. Cut the pork into slices that are about ½-in (1.25-cm) thick by 1-in (2.5-cm) wide, and then set the pork aside.

Bring the liquid in the pot to a boil over high heat. Continue boiling until the liquid reduces to about 1 cup (250 ml) and thickens slightly—depending on how much water was previously added, reducing the sauce may take anywhere from 10–20 minutes. Decrease the heat to low and discard the cinnamon stick, bay leaf, and star anise.

Place the sliced pork into the pot and gently stir and cook until just heated through, 2–3 minutes. Serve with steamed white rice.

GLAZED ROASTED SPAM

If Hawaiians are the top consumers of Spam, I'd venture to guess that Filipinos are a close second. Like many other canned goods that made their way to U.S. troops in the Philippines during World War II and thereafter, Spam ultimately gained popularity among Filipinos and has remained in Filipino cupboards ever since. Served alongside Fast and Simple Garlic Fried Rice (page 53) and eggs, Spam is usually eaten for breakfast in the Philippines. Although I realize that there are a few (Okay, maybe a lot of) people that may turn their noses up at a can of Spam, a quick and easy candy glaze of brown sugar, coffee, and spices creates a nice balance to the Spam's saltiness—a great combination that is sure to win over a few Spam converts.

Serves 4–6
Prep Time: 10 minutes
Cooking Time: 10 minutes

2 tablespoons brown sugar
1 tablespoon brewed hot coffee, or hot water
½ teaspoon freshly ground black pepper
⅛ teaspoon smoked Spanish paprika, or regular paprika
One 12-oz (340-g) can of Spam

Combine the sugar, coffee (or water), black pepper, and paprika in a small bowl and stir until the sugar dissolves.

Position an oven rack about 6 in (15 cm) from the broiler and heat the broiler to high.

Remove the Spam from the can and cut the Spam into ¼-in (6-mm) slices. Place the Spam slices on a sheet pan lined with parchment paper. Brush the brown sugar glaze onto the first side of the Spam slices.

Place the Spam underneath the broiler and broil until the glaze begins to bubble and caramelize and the edges of the Spam begin to brown, 3–5 minutes. Flip the Spam slices over and then brush with the rest of the brown sugar glaze. Broil the second side until the glaze begins to bubble and caramelize, and the edges of the Spam begin to brown, 3–5 minutes more.

Remove the Spam from the broiler and allow to cool slightly. The glaze will harden and become sticky as the Spam cools. Serve the candied Spam with Fast and Simple Garlic Fried Rice and eggs for a Filipino breakfast of *Spamsilog*—see Filipino Breakfast (and Wordplay), page 53.

FILIPINO GARLIC SAUSAGE PATTIES LONGGANISA HUBBAD

Filipino pork sausage, or *longganisa*, come in all shapes and sizes across the Philippine archipelago—some skewing towards the very sweet, and others towards the very sour. This is my version of a Northern Filipino-style sausage—redolent of garlic and sharp vinegar. And because these sausages are in patty form, rather than stuffed into casings, they are referred to as *longganisang hubbad*, or "naked sausage." Be sure to use pork shoulder, and not lean ground pork, for this sausage. Pork shoulder provides the right amount of fat that is needed to keep the sausage moist when cooking. Just ask your butcher to coarsely grind a boneless pork shoulder for you and you'll soon have a perfect mix of pork and fat for sausage making.

Makes 15–18 sausage patties
Prep Time: 20 minutes, plus 4 hours refrigeration
Cooking Time: 15 minutes

½ cup (125 ml) dark Filipino cane vinegar (*sukang iloco*), or cider vinegar
8–10 cloves garlic, finely minced
1½ tablespoons coarse sea salt, or kosher salt
2 tablespoons brown sugar
1 teaspoon smoked Spanish paprika, or regular paprika
1 teaspoon freshly ground black pepper
½ teaspoon dried red pepper flakes
2 lbs (1 kg) coarsely ground pork shoulder
2 tablespoons Annatto Oil (page 26), or regular vegetable oil

In a large bowl whisk together the vinegar, garlic, salt, brown sugar, paprika, black pepper, and red pepper flakes. Add the ground pork to the bowl and gently mix with your hands, or a rubber spatula, until everything is combined. Cover and refrigerate the pork mixture for at least 4 hours, or overnight for a stronger flavored sausage.

Form the pork into patties that are about 3 in (7.5 cm) in diameter and ¼-in (6-mm) thick. At this point you can cover the patties and refrigerate for use within 1 week, or freeze for up to 3 months.

Heat the oil in a large non-stick skillet over medium heat. Working in batches, place the sausage patties into the skillet and gently cook until the sausage is browned on each side and cooked through, about 5–6 minutes per side. If cooking frozen patties, add 1–2 minutes of cooking time per side.

Alternatively, these sausage patties are fantastic when grilled on the barbecue. Just grill the patties over direct high heat until grill marks appear, and then move the patties to a cooler side of the grill to gently finish cooking.

Serve the *longganisa* alongside Tomato Relish with Fish Sauce and Shallots (page 23). Or, serve the *longganisa* with Fast and Simple Garlic Fried Rice and a fried egg for a hearty Filipino *longsilog* breakfast (see page 53 for more information on Filipino breakfast).

> **COOK'S NOTE:** For a great bar snack, set aside 4 uncooked *longganisa* patties for use in my Filipino Scotch Egg recipe (page 111).

SARDINES IN SPICY TOMATO SAUCE

For some Filipinos, myself included, a can of sardines in tomato sauce can qualify as comfort food. In fact, many of my dinners as a college student and bachelor consisted of canned sardines from the Philippines heated through in a skillet and then dumped on a pile of rice.

Although I have fond memories of those simple dinners, I've found that I can easily replicate them not by opening a can, but by using fresh ingredients instead.

Fresh sardines are inexpensive, sustainable, and are becoming easier to find as they rise in popularity—though they are easiest to find in Asian markets. The sardines can simply be placed atop a freshly made sauce of tomato paste, white wine, and cherry tomatoes, and then quickly finished underneath the broiler. Despite my love of canned sardines, I've not opened a single tin since making this recipe.

Serves 4–6
Prep Time: 15 minutes
Cooking Time: 35 minutes

2 tablespoons, plus 3 tablespoons
   olive oil
2 large shallots, minced (2 tablespoons)
4 cloves garlic, minced (1 tablespoon)
½ teaspoon dried red pepper flakes
½ teaspoon smoked Spanish paprika,
   or regular paprika
1 tablespoon tomato paste
1 lb (500 g) cherry tomatoes, halved
½ cup (125 ml) white wine
¼ cup (65 ml) water
1 tablespoon fish sauce
8–10 small fresh sardines, about
   1 lb (500 g), cleaned and gutted
2 teaspoons salt
1 teaspoon freshly ground black pepper
1 tablespoon fresh *calamansi* juice,
   or fresh lemon juice
Fresh *calamansi* limes, or fresh lemon
   wedges, for squeezing over the
   sardines

Heat 2 tablespoons of the olive oil in a large oven-proof sauté pan over moderately high heat. Add the shallot, garlic, dried red pepper flakes, and paprika and cook until the shallot becomes soft and translucent, 3–5 minutes. Add the tomato paste and stir to combine, continuing to cook until the tomato paste just begins to brown, 1 minute more.

Toss the cherry tomatoes into the pan and sauté until the tomatoes soften and have released some of their juices, 5–7 minutes.

Pour the wine into the pan, stirring to scrape up any browned bits from the bottom of the pan. Add the water and fish sauce and simmer until the liquid reduces and thickens a bit, about 5 minutes more. Remove from heat and set aside.

Season the sardines, inside and out, with the salt and black pepper. In a large bowl, whisk together the remaining 3 tablespoons of olive oil with the *calamansi* (or lemon) juice. Using your hands, toss the sardines in the olive oil and citrus mixture, making sure the mixture dresses the fish inside and out.

Place an oven rack in the closest position to the broiler and turn the broiler on high heat.

Remove the sardines from the bowl and arrange them in a single layer on top of the tomato sauce in the sauté pan. Place the pan underneath the broiler and broil for 10–12 minutes, flipping the fish over once. The sardines are ready when the skin is nicely browned and crisped, and the thickest part of the fish easily flakes from the tip of a knife.

Serve with steamed white rice and *calamansi* limes, or lemon wedges, on the side for squeezing over the fish.

STUFFED AND GRILLED WHOLE TROUT

A snap to prepare, this recipe is based on a similar dish of stuffed and grilled milkfish I encountered in the Philippines a few years ago. Although this recipe calls for trout, you can easily substitute any mild, firm-fleshed fish that is locally available and inexpensive. The real key lies in the stuffing for the fish—a flavorful mix of tomato, shallot, and green onion soaked in soy sauce and *calamansi* (or lemon) juice. Wrapping the fish in banana leaves not only helps to keep the fish and stuffing intact, but it also lends a smoky and grassy aroma to the fish.

Serves 4 as part of a multi-course meal
Prep Time: 20 minutes
Cooking Time: 20 minutes

1 large tomato, diced
2 shallots, minced
1 green onion (scallion), trimmed and thinly sliced (white and green parts)
2 tablespoons soy sauce
2 tablespoons fresh *calamansi* juice, or fresh lemon juice
2 whole trout (1–2 lbs/500 g–1 kg each), cleaned and gutted
2 tablespoons oil
Salt, to taste
Freshly ground black pepper, to taste
Banana leaves, or foil, for wrapping

In a small bowl, combine the tomato, shallot, green onion, soy sauce, and *calamansi* juice.

Brush the outside of the trout with the oil, and then season the trout, inside and out, with the salt and pepper. Spoon the tomato mixture into the cavities of the trout. Any unused tomato mixture can be reserved as a dipping sauce for the fish.

Clean and oil the grates of your grill and preheat for direct high-heat grilling.

Place each fish on the center of a banana leaf large enough to enclose the entire fish. Wrap the banana leaves over each fish, making sure to fold over the open ends. Secure the banana leaf with kitchen twine, wrapping and tying the leaf around the fish like a package. Alternatively, you can simply wrap the fish in aluminum foil.

Place the wrapped fish on the hot grill and cook for 15–20 minutes, turning the fish over once. During this time the banana leaves will char and some juices may leak out—this is normal and will lend to the smoky flavor of the fish.

Remove the fish from the grill and rest the fish for 5–10 minutes. Using a sharp knife or kitchen shears, cut open the banana leaf package. Serve the fish with steamed white rice.

BROILED MACKEREL FILLETS

The combination of vinegar, soy, garlic, and black pepper can be used to great effect outside the confines of an *adobo*. The ubiquitous Filipino mixture is also often used to marinate milkfish (the national fish of the Philippines), which is then deep-fried to a crisp.

While I do love milkfish (especially its fatty belly), its hundreds of pin bones often make me think twice about cooking with it. Which is why I now soak mackerel fillets in the vinegar-soy marinade instead of milkfish.

Mackerel is not only full-flavored and fatty, but it's also a sustainable source of seafood. And rather than deep-frying, broiling the mackerel is a healthier, faster and less messy alternative.

Serves 4 as part of a multi-course meal
Prep Time: 10 minutes, plus at least 1 hour to marinate
Cooking Time: 10 minutes

½ cup (125 ml) white Filipino cane vinegar, or rice vinegar
¼ cup (65 ml) soy sauce
6 cloves garlic, smashed with the side of a knife and peeled
½ teaspoon freshly ground black pepper
4 fresh skin-on mackerel fillets, about 6 oz (175 g) each, scaled and deboned
2 tablespoons oil
Coarse salt
Fresh coriander leaves (cilantro), roughly chopped, for garnish

Combine the vinegar, soy sauce, garlic, and black pepper in a small bowl. Place the mackerel fillets in a shallow baking dish and pour the marinade over the fish. Cover the baking dish with plastic wrap and marinate the fish for at least 1 hour in the refrigerator.

Position an oven rack about 6 in (15 cm) from the broiler and heat the broiler to high.

Remove the fish from the marinade and pat dry with paper towels. Discard the marinade. Rub the oil all over the fillets to coat well. Place the fillets, skin-side up, on a baking sheet lined with foil. Sprinkle the skin with coarse salt, and then place the fish underneath the broiler. Broil the fish, without turning, until the skin is lightly browned and the flesh flakes easily from the tip of a knife, 5–7 minutes. Remove the fish from the broiler and garnish with the coriander leaves. Serve immediately.

FILIPINO-STYLE FRIED CHICKEN

Like many other American foods that became popular in the Philippines, fried chicken arose from the GI camps present throughout the archipelago following World War II. Also like many other American foods that became popular in the Philippines, fried chicken was quickly adapted to suit the particular tastes of the Filipino.

For that familiar salty-sour combination that Filipinos love so much, chicken pieces destined for the fryer are often marinated in a mixture of soy sauce, vinegar, and *calamansi* juice. And like its American counterpart, Filipino-Style Fried Chicken can be dredged in flour and buttermilk for extra crunch and texture. But rather than using buttermilk, I use coconut milk for an extra dimension of flavor. After the chicken emerges from the hot oil, it is tender and juicy on the inside, and wonderfully crispy and subtly coconutty on the outside.

Serves 4–6 as part of a multi-course meal
Prep Time: 20 minutes, plus overnight to marinate
Cooking Time: 45 minutes

½ cup (125 ml) soy sauce
¼ cup (65 ml) cane vinegar, or white distilled vinegar
¼ cup (65 ml) fresh *calamansi* juice, or fresh lemon juice
6 cloves garlic, smashed with the side of a knife and peeled
1 large whole chicken, cut into 8 pieces
1½ cups (375 g) all-purpose flour
2 teaspoons freshly ground black pepper
2 teaspoons salt
1 cup (250 ml) canned unsweetened coconut milk
High-heat cooking oil, for frying

Combine the soy sauce, vinegar, *calamansi* juice, and garlic in a large zip-top bag. Place the chicken pieces into the bag and marinate in the refrigerator overnight.

Remove the chicken from the marinade and then pat dry with paper towels. In a shallow rimmed dish, mix together the flour, black pepper, and salt. Pour the coconut milk into a large bowl.

Dredge the chicken pieces in the flour mixture, shaking off any excess flour. Dip and coat each floured piece of chicken in the coconut milk, allowing any excess coconut milk to drip back into the bowl. Dredge the chicken in a second coating of flour, again shaking off any excess flour. Place the coated chicken pieces on a cooling rack and rest for 5–10 minutes. This resting period allows the coating on the chicken to set and will result in a crispier texture when fried.

In a large heavy skillet, pour in the oil to reach a depth of about ½ in (1.25 cm). Heat the oil over medium heat until it reaches 325°F (160°C) on a deep fry thermometer.

Working in two batches, gently place the chicken, skin side down, into the oil. Fry each batch of chicken until golden brown on each side, 10–12 minutes per side. Be sure to adjust the heat to maintain the temperature of the oil between 300°F (150°C) and 325°F (160°C).

Transfer the chicken to a sheet pan lined with paper towels. Serve warm.

CRISPY PAN-FRIED SALMON WITH SWEET AND SOUR RELISH
ESCABECHE

Filipino *escabeche* usually features a whole deep-fried fish smothered in a sweet and sour sauce studded with bell peppers. While I love the flavor and texture of most anything that's been dunked in bubbling hot oil, deep-frying a whole fish at home can be a messy endeavor.

So for a neater, and healthier, version of *escabeche*, salmon fillets can be placed skin-side down in a very hot, oil-slicked skillet and seared just until the skin is crisp. A sweet and sour pan sauce can then quickly be made in the same skillet. The addition of diced mangoes to the sauce lends a welcome layer of freshness and sweetness to the sauce.

Serves 4
Prep Time: 25 minutes
Cooking Time: 25 minutes

Four 1-in (2.5-cm) thick skin-on salmon fillets, about 6 oz (175 g) each, scaled and deboned
4 tablespoons high-heat cooking oil, divided
Salt, to taste
Freshly ground black pepper, to taste
1 small red onion, diced
1 small green bell pepper, deseeded and diced
1 small red bell pepper, deseeded and diced
4 cloves garlic, minced
One 1-in (2.5-cm) piece fresh ginger, peeled and minced
½ cup (125 ml), plus 1 tablespoon water
¼ cup (65 ml) Filipino cane vinegar, or white distilled vinegar
1 tablespoon fish sauce
1 tablespoon brown sugar
1 teaspoon cornstarch
1 ripe mango, peeled, deseeded and diced
2 green onions (scallions), thinly sliced (white and green parts)

Brush the salmon fillets all over with 2 tablespoons of oil. Season each side of the salmon fillets with the salt and black pepper.

Heat the remaining 2 tablespoons of oil in a large skillet over moderately high heat until the oil is almost smoking. Tilt the pan to ensure that the entire bottom surface is slicked with oil. Place the salmon, skin-side down, into the hot pan. Cook the salmon, undisturbed, until the skin is very crispy, 4–5 minutes. Resist any urge to poke, prod, or flip the salmon while the skin is crisping!

Flip the salmon and cook until the flesh side is seared, 1–2 minutes for medium-rare depending on the thickness of the fish. Place the salmon, skin-side up, on a large platter and loosely tent with foil. Set aside to rest.

Add the onion and bell pepper to the pan and sauté until the onion softens and becomes translucent, 3–5 minutes. Add the garlic and ginger, and cook until very fragrant, 1–2 minutes. Stir in ½ a cup of the water, along with the vinegar, fish sauce, and brown sugar, stirring to scrape up any browned bits from the bottom of the pan.

Combine the cornstarch with the remaining 1 tablespoon of water and then stir the mixture into the pan. Bring everything to a boil, and then reduce the heat to low and simmer until the sauce thickens, about 5 minutes. Add the mangoes and cook until the mangoes are just heated through, 1–2 minutes.

Spoon the sauce onto individual plates, and then place the salmon fillets, skin-side up, on top. Garnish with the green onion. Serve with steamed white rice.

GRILLED TURKEY BURGERS TURKEY INASAL BURGERS

This is my fun take on traditional Grilled Lemongrass Chicken (chicken *inasal*, page 84), but in burger form. With bits of lemongrass and ginger, the flavors of chicken *inasal* are echoed in every bite of these moist turkey burgers—especially when topped with a slaw of Pickled Green Papaya (page 22). Additional flavor is added to the patties in the form of Homemade Mayonnaise (page 25), though store-bought mayonnaise can also be used. Mixing the mayonnaise into the patties themselves not only adds flavor, but it keeps the turkey moist as well.

Makes 4 burgers
Prep Time: 25 minutes
Cooking Time: 10 minutes

1 lb (500 g) ground turkey meat
1 stalk lemongrass, bottom 4–6 in (10–15 cm) minced
½-in (1.25-cm) piece fresh ginger, minced
1 clove garlic, minced
½ teaspoon freshly ground black pepper
1 tablespoon brown sugar
1 tablespoon soy sauce
1 teaspoon fish sauce
2 tablespoons Homemade Mayonnaise (page 25), or regular store-bought mayonnaise, plus more for spreading onto buns
4 hamburger buns
Homemade Banana Ketchup (page 24), or store-bought banana ketchup, for spreading onto buns
Lettuce
Pickled Green Papaya (page 22) for topping

Make the Homemade Mayonnaise, Homemade Banana Ketchup, and Pickled Green Papaya by following their recipes on pages 25, 24, and 22.

Clean and oil the grates of your grill and preheat for direct high-heat grilling.

Combine the turkey, lemongrass, ginger, garlic, black pepper, brown sugar, soy sauce, fish sauce, and Homemade Mayonnaise in a large bowl. Using your hands, or a rubber spatula, gently mix the ingredients in the bowl until fully incorporated.

Divide the meat mixture into four equal portions, and then form each portion into a patty about a ½-in (1.25-cm) thick.

Grill the burgers until cooked through and nicely charred on each side, 4–5 minutes per side, or until an instant-read thermometer registers 165°F (75°C) when inserted into the meat.

Slather the hamburger buns with more Homemade Mayonnaise and Homemade Banana Ketchup. Place lettuce on each hamburger bun bottom, and then nestle the turkey burgers onto the lettuce. Top each burger with some Pickled Green Papaya, and then cover with the top bun. Serve Immediately.

GRILLED PORK CHOPS WITH FIRE-ROASTED PEPPERS AND SPICY COCONUT SAUCE
BICOL EXPRESS

The Bicol region of the Philippines is known for its predilection to coconut milk and chili peppers as many of the regional dishes there feature both ingredients. But perhaps the most famous of all Bicolano eats is the dish known as "Bicol express." Named after the train that traveled between Manila and Legazpi City, Bicol express is typically comprised of pork cooked in a fiery sauce made from the aforementioned coconut milk and chili peppers. As with all Filipino dishes, however, every household in Bicol has a different preparation of the namesake dish. There are variants that use ground pork, while others use pork belly. And there are versions that are salted with fermented shrimp paste, while others use dried anchovies. The combinations are endless. My rendition of Bicol express features thick-cut pork chops that are marinated in coconut milk and then grilled alongside fresh chili peppers. The grilled chops are then finished off with a fragrant and spicy coconut sauce. Although the coconut sauce does have a hint of heat, diners can take an even faster track to Bicol with a bite or two of the fire-roasted chili peppers.

Serves 4
Prep Time: 20 minutes, plus at least 4 hours to marinate
Cooking Time: 20 minutes

1 cup (250 ml) unsweetened canned coconut milk
½ cup (125 ml) soy sauce
2 lemongrass stalks, bottom 4–6 in (10–15 cm) trimmed and finely minced
½ teaspoon dried red pepper flakes
2 tablespoons brown sugar
4 bone-in, 1-in (2.5-cm) thick pork chops, about 6–8 oz (175–250 g) each
6–8 red and green jalapeño chili peppers, or serrano chili peppers, or a mixture of both

For the Spicy Coconut Sauce:
1 tablespoon high-heat cooking oil
1 tablespoon minced shallot
1 tablespoon minced garlic
One 1-in (2.5-cm) piece fresh ginger, peeled and minced
1 cup (250 ml) unsweetened canned coconut milk
1 teaspoon fish sauce, plus more, to taste
1 teaspoon brown sugar
1–2 teaspoons *sambal oelek* chili paste (optional)

Combine the coconut milk with the soy sauce, lemongrass, red pepper flakes, and the brown sugar in a medium bowl. Nestle the pork chops into a shallow baking dish, and then pour the marinade over the pork chops. Turn the pork chops to ensure they are evenly coated in the marinade. Marinate the pork chops in the refrigerator for at least 4 hours, or overnight, turning them over once to ensure even marination.

Clean and oil the grates of your grill and preheat for direct high-heat grilling.

Remove the pork chops from the marinade and discard the marinade. Place the pork chops on a hot, cleaned and oiled grill and grill for 3–4 minutes per side, or until an instant-read thermometer registers 145°F (63°C) when inserted into the meat. Grill the chili peppers, turning often, until charred and tender, 5–10 minutes total depending on the size of the chili peppers.

Remove the pork chops and chili peppers from the grill and allow to rest for at least 10 minutes.

Meanwhile, make the Spicy Coconut Sauce by heating a large wok or sauté pan over high heat until a drop of water sizzles and evaporates on contact. Swirl the oil into the pan, and then add the shallot, garlic, and ginger, and stir-fry until the garlic just begins to brown, about 30 seconds. Add the coconut milk, along with the fish sauce, brown sugar, and chili paste (if using). Simmer for 2 minutes more and taste the sauce. Season with additional fish sauce as needed and remove from the heat.

Serve the pork chops with rice and drizzle with the Spicy Coconut Sauce. Garnish with the fire-roasted chili peppers.

CHAPTER 6

FILIPINO FINGER FOODS AND COCKTAILS
PULUTAN

The term "*pulutan*" is derived from the Filipino word "*pulot*" which literally translates as "to pick up with the fingers." As such, *pulutan* traditionally refers to small bites and finger foods that are best served alongside an alcoholic drink. What can I say? Filipinos love to drink. Of course, any or all of the delicious *tapas*-style delicacies in this section can be served as an appetizer without need for booze. Likewise, anything from the Appetizers section can also be served as *pulutan* with drink in hand. It's a fine line between appetizers and bar food—a line probably stumbled over after a few beers or cocktails.

Although definitely not a hard and fast rule, the distinction I like to make between *pulutan* and appetizers is that *pulutan* are generally found from street vendors or bars throughout the Philippines, whereas appetizers are more commonly prepared at home—but armed with the recipes in this section, you can now make *pulutan* at home too! And while a cold San Miguel beer from the Philippines is *de rigueur* with *pulutan*, I also provide a small selection of refreshing cocktails to quench your thirst. In fact, there is a very rich history of vintage Philippine-born cocktails, as well as Tiki drinks created by Filipino-Americans in post-prohibition Hollywood. Although these vintage cocktails and Tiki drinks may require various spirits and special syrups, they are a great way to look back and experience a bit of Filipino culinary and cultural history. And besides, nothing helps you travel through time better than a cocktail.

GRILLED CHICKEN TROTTERS ADIDAS

The menus of Chinese *dim sum* joints often offer meltingly tender chicken feet under the moniker of "phoenix claws." But the Chinese aren't the only clever marketers of this unusual delicacy.

In some parts of the Philippines, street vendors can be found grilling marinated chicken feet that are playfully nicknamed "*adidas*" (the three toes standing in for the three stripes of the famous shoe brand). Rather than being soft and tender like its Chinese counterpart, this grilled Filipino-style of chicken feet is delectably chewy. My interpretation of this popular Filipino street food is a spicy-sweet rendition that goes perfect with a cold beer.

Chicken feet can be easily found in many Asian markets, and are also showing up in larger supermarkets such as Whole Foods. However, if you're still chicken about chicken feet, don't fret—this spicy marinade works wonderfully well with chicken wings too.

Serves 4–6 as a snack
Prep Time: 10 minutes, plus at least 4 hours to marinate
Cooking Time: 45 minutes

1 lb (500 g) chicken feet
½ cup (125 ml) fresh or canned pineapple juice
¼ cup (65 ml) soy sauce
¼ cup (65 ml) Filipino coconut vinegar, or white distilled vinegar
One 1-in (2.5-cm) piece fresh ginger, peeled and minced
4 cloves garlic, minced
1 tablespoon oil
1 tablespoon *sambal oelek* chili paste
1 tablespoon brown sugar

Place the chicken feet in a small pot and add enough water to cover the chicken feet by 1 in (2.5 cm). Place the pot over high heat and bring to a boil, and then cover and simmer over low heat for 30 minutes.

Drain the chicken feet into a large colander set in the sink, and then rinse the chicken feet with cold running water until they are cool enough to handle. Transfer the chicken feet to a cutting board. Using a sharp knife, cut off and discard the tips of each claw by slicing through the first joint. If there are any black spots or scaly patches of skin on the "palms" of the chicken feet, remove those with a knife as well.

Combine the rest of the ingredients in a small bowl and whisk until the brown sugar is dissolved. Place the trimmed chicken feet into a large resealable food storage bag, and then pour in the marinade. Marinate the chicken for at least 4 hours, or overnight, in the refrigerator.

Preheat the grill for direct high-heat grilling.

Remove the chicken feet from the marinade and place on a hot, cleaned and oiled grill grate. Grill the chicken feet, turning often, until they are nicely charred on all sides, 5–8 minutes total.

Serve the chicken feet with some Pickled Green Papaya (page 22) on the side, or some Spicy Pickled Peppers (page 20).

GRILLED PORK SKEWERS INIHAW NA BABOY

Barbecued pork skewers varnished in a sticky-sweet glaze are a well-known snack and street food throughout the Philippines. What isn't as well-known though, is the secret barbecue ingredient used by many a Pinoy grill master.

That secret ingredient? Lemon-lime soda. It's true. Some Filipinos swear by Sprite, and others 7UP, but any can of your favorite lemon-lime soda adds sweetness and tang to the marinade for this pork. And when the marinade is reduced down to a thick syrup, it gives these skewers their trademark sticky coating—ready to be washed down with a cold beer.

Serves 4–6
Prep Time: 25 minutes, plus overnight to marinate
Cooking Time: 20 minutes

1 stalk lemongrass, bottom 4–6 in (10–15 cm) trimmed and minced
One 2-in (5-cm) piece of fresh ginger, peeled and minced
5–6 cloves garlic, minced
1 teaspoon dried red pepper flakes
½ cup (90 g) brown sugar
½ cup (125 ml) soy sauce
One 12-oz (355-ml) can lemon-lime soda
2 lbs (1 kg) pork shoulder, sliced into thin strips
15–20 bamboo skewers

In a large bowl, combine the lemongrass, ginger, garlic, red pepper flakes, brown sugar, soy sauce, and soda and stir until the sugar is dissolved. Pour half of the marinade into a small container or bowl, and then cover and set aside in the refrigerator.

Place the pork in a large shallow baking dish and pour in the other half of the marinade. Cover the pork and refrigerate overnight.

To prevent the bamboo skewers from scorching, soak them in water for at least 30 minutes.

Preheat the grill for direct high heat grilling.

Pour the reserved unused half of the marinade into a small pot over high heat. Bring the marinade to a boil and cook, stirring constantly, until it reduces into a glaze and has a thick syrup consistency, 5–10 minutes. Remove the glaze from the heat and set aside to cool slightly.

Meanwhile, remove the pork from the marinade and discard the marinade. Thread the pork onto the skewers so that the meat is evenly spaced and spread across the skewer. Place the skewers on the hot grill and brush with the glaze. Grill the pork, while brushing with the glaze and turning frequently, for 7–8 minutes or until the pork is cooked through and nicely glazed and charred.

GARLIC LEMONGRASS SHRIMP

My cousin, Kathy, first prepared this dish for me a few years ago, and since that time, I've learned that cooking shrimp in 7UP or Sprite is a popular method in some parts of the Philippines.

I imagine that this way of cooking is a play on Chinese drunken shrimp that are usually cooked in beer. But since Filipinos would rather drink their beer than use it in a marinade, soda was used instead—at least that's what I like to think. The result is a savory-sweet sauce made fragrant with shallot, garlic and lemongrass that all meld perfectly with the rich head-on shrimp. These sweet shrimp are especially good when enjoyed with a cold beer. Be sure to suck on the shrimp heads too.

If you'd rather not use head-on, shell-on shrimp, you can use peeled shrimp instead—the sauce will still be delicious, but it will lack the rich shrimp flavor imparted by the shrimp heads and shells.

Serves 4 as a snack
Prep Time: 15 minutes, plus 1 hour to marinate
Cooking Time: 10 minutes

One 12-oz (355-ml) can lemon-lime soda
1 lb (500 g) fresh or previously frozen head-on, shell-on medium shrimp
2 tablespoons high-heat cooking oil
1 tablespoon minced shallot
1 tablespoon minced garlic
1 stalk lemongrass, bottom 4–6 in (10–15 cm) trimmed and finely minced
¼ teaspoon dried red pepper flakes, plus more, to taste
1 teaspoon fish sauce
1 tablespoon butter
Salt, to taste
Freshly ground black pepper, to taste

Combine the soda and shrimp in a large bowl and marinate the shrimp for 1 hour in the refrigerator.

Heat a large wok or sauté pan over high heat until a drop of water sizzles and evaporates on contact. Swirl in the oil and add the shallot, garlic, lemongrass, and red pepper flakes. Cook until the garlic just begins to brown, about 30 seconds.

Add the soda and the shrimp, stirring to scrape up any browned bits from the bottom of the pan. Add the fish sauce and bring everything to a boil, stirring frequently until the shrimp are pink and cooked through, 3–4 minutes. Using a slotted spoon, transfer the cooked shrimp to a large platter.

Continue boiling the liquid until it is reduced by half and thickens slightly, 3–5 minutes. Add the butter and stir until melted, and then season the sauce to taste with salt and pepper. Drizzle the sauce over the shrimp and serve immediately, either with steamed white rice, or with crusty bread, for sopping up the sauce.

CRISPY CHICKEN WINGS WITH SPICY ADOBO GLAZE
CARABAO WINGS

I first developed this recipe for my blog some years ago. After receiving much positive feedback from my readers, I went on to serve these wings from my gourmet Filipino food truck, The Manila Machine. As such, this recipe is both blog-tested and road-tested. As a nod and a wink to spicy Buffalo wings, I dubbed my spicy chicken wings as "*carabao* wings"—the Filipino water buffalo is called a *carabao*. Next to my Spicy Sizzling Pork Platter (*sisig*, page 112), these wings were Manila Machine best sellers whenever I'd park the truck near bars and breweries, and with good reason—with a fiery afterburn that begs for a cold beer, these wings make for a great bar snack.

Serves 4 as a snack
Prep Time: 10 minutes
Cooking Time: 30 minutes

2 tablespoons butter
1 bay leaf
4 cloves garlic, minced
1–2 Thai chili peppers, thinly sliced (optional)
¼ teaspoon dried red pepper flakes
⅓ cup (80 ml) apple cider vinegar
2 tablespoons soy sauce
2 tablespoons brown sugar
½ teaspoon freshly ground black pepper
¼ teaspoon coarse salt
Oil, for frying
2 lbs (1 kg) chicken wings

Place the butter and bay leaf in a small saucepan over medium heat and stir until the butter melts. After the butter has melted and begins to foam, add the garlic, chili pepper (if using), and pepper flakes and cook just until the garlic begins to brown, 1–2 minutes.

Pour in the vinegar and soy sauce, stirring to scrape up any browned bits from the bottom of the pan. Add the brown sugar, black pepper and salt and stir to combine. Bring the mixture to a boil, and then reduce the heat to low and simmer, stirring occasionally, until the mixture reduces and thickens into a glaze, 7–10 minutes. Remove the glaze from the heat and set aside.

In a large heavy skillet, pour in the oil to reach a depth of about ½ in (1.25 cm). Heat the oil over medium heat until it reaches 375°F (190°C) on a deep fry thermometer. Fry the wings in batches, until golden brown, about 10 minutes total. Drain the wings on paper towels.

After all the wings are fried, place them into a large bowl. Pour the glaze over the chicken wings and toss to coat. Discard the bay leaf. Serve immediately.

BARBECUED PIG'S EARS WALKMAN

Although "nose-to-tail" eating has been gaining in popularity in many high-end restaurants these days, Filipinos (along with many other cultures) have long appreciated the virtues of eating whole-hog. Among the many offal offerings from street vendors in the Philippines, grilled pig's ears are often a favorite bar snack. And much like the playfully named "*adidas*" chicken feet (page 104), pig's ears are given the ironic moniker, "Walkman," in reference to the popular earphones from the '80s. You can find fresh pig's ears at Asian and Latin markets, and from gourmet online meat purveyors as well. After a long simmer on the stovetop, the ears become tender and are ready to be finished on a hot grill. I like to make a quick sweet and sour glaze for the ears since they can still take up so many flavors on the grill. The final dish highlights each porky aspect of the ears as tender chewy cartilage is sandwiched between layers of crispy charred skin and meat—a unique, yet rich and flavorful treat.

Serves 2–4 as a snack
Prep Time: 20 minutes
Cooking Time: 2 hours, 30 minutes

2 large fresh pig's ears
Water, to cover
4 cloves garlic, pressed with the side of a knife and peeled
2 bay leaves
1 teaspoon whole black peppercorns
½ cup (125 ml) fresh or canned pineapple juice
¼ cup (65 ml) fresh *calamansi* juice, or fresh lime juice
1 tablespoon brown sugar
1 teaspoon freshly ground black pepper

If the pig's ears still have any bristles on them, singe the bristles off by passing the pig's ears over the burner on the stove. Place the pig's ears in a large pot and pour in enough water to just cover the pig's ears. Place the pot over high heat and bring to a boil. Boil the pig's ears for 5 minutes to remove any impurities, and then drain the ears into a large colander and rinse with cold running water. Rinse the pot out as well.

Return the pig's ears to the large pot and add the garlic, bay leaves and whole black peppercorns. Pour in enough cold water to just cover the pig's ears. Place the pot over high heat and bring to a boil. Cover the pot, reduce the heat to low and simmer for at least 2 hours or until the ears are very tender and a fork can easily pierce through them.

Gently remove the ears from the liquid, taking care not to tear the tender skin, and set aside to cool. You can strain and reserve the pork stock for another use—it will keep refrigerated for up to a week, or up to 3 months in the freezer.

While the ears are cooling, add the pineapple juice, *calamansi* (or lime) juice, brown sugar, and ground black pepper to a small pot. Place the pot over high heat and bring to a boil. Continue boiling until the liquid thickens slightly and reduces by half, 5–10 minutes. Set the glaze aside.

Clean and oil the grates of your grill and prepare it for direct medium-heat cooking. Because the skin on the pig's ears is very sticky and gelatinous, it is very important to preheat, clean and oil the grill grates on the barbecue to prevent the ears from sticking.

Brush some of the glaze on both sides of the pig's ears, and then lay the pig's ears on the hot grill grates. Grill the pig's ears, basting often with the glaze, until the ears are nicely charred and grill marks appear, 5–8 minutes per side.

Transfer the grilled pig's ears to a cutting board and immediately cut the ears into thin slices. Serve the grilled pig's ears with cold beer.

COOK'S NOTE: Instead of grilling, you can also deep-fry the pig's ears. After the pig's ears have simmered in the water for at least 2 hours, dry them well with paper towels, dredge them in rice flour, and fry in hot oil. Just be careful as the oil will splatter from the moisture in the ears.

PAN-SEARED GARLIC RIB EYE STEAK SALPICAO

The origins of this popular Filipino bar snack are little known, but it can perhaps be traced back to Portugal by way of Spain. The Spanish term "*salpicado*" translates to "splattered," which may relate to the way in which the garlic and beef in this recipe are cooked in hot oil. Whereas the Portuguese dish known as "*salpicao*" consists of pork sausage, it has no resemblance to the Filipino dish of the same name. No matter the origins, Filipino *salpicao* is delicious in its own right, featuring a heavy dose of fried garlic sprinkled atop juicy beef. My version uses rib eye steaks cooked medium-rare and drizzled in a soy and bourbon sauce quickly made from the pan drippings.

Serves 4 as a snack
Prep Time: 5 minutes
Cooking Time: 20 minutes

1 tablespoon high-heat cooking oil
2 tablespoons minced garlic
Two 1-in (2.5-cm) thick boneless rib eye
   steaks (about 8–10 oz/250–330 g, each)
Salt, to taste
Freshly ground black pepper, to taste
¼ teaspoon smoked Spanish paprika, or
   regular paprika
½ cup (125 ml) water
1 tablespoon soy sauce
¼ cup (65 ml) bourbon whiskey
Pinch of sugar

Heat the oil in a large heavy skillet (preferably cast iron) over moderately high heat. Add the garlic to the skillet and sauté until the garlic becomes golden brown, 1–2 minutes. Leaving the oil in the skillet, transfer the garlic to a small plate lined with a paper towel and set aside. Leave the skillet over moderately high heat so it can properly sear the steaks.

Season the steaks all over with the salt, pepper and paprika. Place the steaks into the hot skillet and sear until nicely browned and crusty on both sides, 7–10 minutes total for medium-rare steaks. Transfer the steaks to a large platter and set aside to rest for at least 10 minutes.

Meanwhile, pour the water and soy sauce into the skillet, stirring to scrape up any browned bits from the bottom of the pan. Continue to cook for 2–3 minutes more until the water reduces by about half. Turn off the heat and add the bourbon to the skillet. Using a long match, or a long-handled stick lighter, carefully ignite the bourbon and allow the flames to subside and burn out. The flames should die down in less than a minute.

Transfer the rested steaks to a cutting board, and then pour any accumulated juices from the platter and into the skillet. Return the skillet to high heat, and then stir in the sugar and simmer the sauce for 2–3 minutes more just to heat it through. Remove the skillet from the heat.

Cut the steaks into bite-sized cubes, drizzle with the sauce, and sprinkle with the reserved fried garlic. Provide toothpicks or cocktail forks with the cubed steak. Serve immediately with a sliced crusty baguette for sopping up any extra sauce.

COOK'S NOTE: You can also serve the steaks whole, with rice, as a meal for two.

CRISPY CHICKEN LIVERS PRITONG ATAY

I once heard that eating chicken livers with beer or liquor helps to stave off the ill-effects of said beer or liquor, because, well, you've got some extra liver in your system to filter the alcohol. I'm not sure if there's any truth to that, but I do know that rich chicken livers are delicious when paired with a cold beer or cocktail. This fact is not lost in the American South, where fried chicken livers are a popular appetizer and bar snack, nor is it lost in the Philippines, where skewered and grilled chicken livers are sold from street vendors and usually washed down with a cold beer. Although I prefer the deep-fried variety of chicken livers, I specifically prefer my grandmother's method of coating the livers in a simple dredge of rice flour and *panko* bread crumbs. After a dunk in Garlic Vinegar Dipping Sauce or Homemade Banana Ketchup these crispy chicken livers are spectacular with or without an alcohol chaser.

Serves 2–4 as a snack
Prep Time: 25 minutes
Cooking Time: 15 minutes

1 lb (500 g) chicken livers, rinsed and drained
2 large eggs
½ cup (about 60 g) rice flour
1½ cups (350 g) *panko* bread crumbs
Oil, for frying
Salt, to taste
Freshly ground black pepper, to taste

Using a sharp knife, cut the livers in half and trim off any fat. Beat the eggs in a small bowl. Place the rice flour in a wide shallow dish, and place the bread crumbs in another wide shallow dish.

Working in batches, gently dredge a few livers at a time in the rice flour, shaking off any excess rice flour. Dip the rice flour-coated livers in the beaten eggs, and then roll them in the bread crumbs to coat. Transfer the coated livers to a large plate.

Pour the oil into a large heavy skillet to reach a depth of 1 in (2.5 cm). Heat over moderately high heat until the oil reaches 350°F (175°C) on a deep fry thermometer. Alternatively, you can drop a few bread crumbs into the hot oil; if the bread crumbs immediately sizzle and begin to brown, the oil is hot enough and ready for frying.

Fry the livers in batches until golden brown, turning once to ensure even cooking, 4–5 minutes total. Transfer the livers to a large plate lined with paper towels and season with salt and pepper.

Serve the livers with Garlic Vinegar Dipping Sauce (page 23) or Homemade Banana Ketchup (page 24).

FILIPINO SCOTCH EGGS SCOTCH-SILOG

Whoever said that the English can't cook, never had a Scotch egg. Scotch eggs are an English bar snack comprised of a hard-boiled egg that is encased in sausage, coated in bread crumbs and deep-fried. My version of Scotch eggs features a soft-boiled egg encased in Filipino Garlic Sausage Patties (*longganisa*—page 93) that is then dredged in rice flour, coated in *panko* bread crumbs and then deep fried. And because my Filipino Scotch Eggs contain sausage, rice, and eggs, it's almost like a Filipino breakfast (see page 53) masquerading as a bar snack!

Serves 4–6 as a snack
Prep Time: 25 minutes
Cooking Time: 10 minutes

6 large eggs (still in the shell)
4 fresh *longganisa* sausage patties (page 93), about ¾ lb (350 g) total
½ cup (about 60 g) rice flour
1 cup (250 g) *panko* bread crumbs
Oil, for frying
Salt, to taste

Place 4 of the eggs into a medium saucepan (leaving the remaining 2 eggs uncooked). Add enough cold water to the pan to cover the 4 eggs and then place the saucepan over high heat. As soon as the water comes to a boil, remove the pan from the heat, and then cover and let stand for 5 minutes for a soft-boiled egg. Carefully drain the eggs, and then place them in a bowl of ice water to cool. Gently crack the eggs all over on a flat surface, and then carefully peel and discard the shells.

Flatten each sausage patty into an oblong disc that is wider and longer than an egg and is about ⅛-in (3-mm) to ¼-in (6-mm) thick. It's important to flatten the sausage into a thin disc so that it can completely envelop an egg, as well as to ensure that the meat cooks quickly and evenly.

Place a soft-boiled egg onto each flattened patty, and then wrap the eggs in the sausage, making sure that the eggs are completely enclosed. Gently roll the meat-covered egg between your hands to smooth the surface of the sausage.

Crack open and beat the remaining 2 uncooked eggs in a small bowl. Place the rice flour in a wide, shallow dish, and place the bread crumbs in another wide, shallow dish.

Gently roll the sausage-wrapped eggs in the rice flour, shake off the excess, and then dredge in the beaten eggs, and then roll in the bread crumbs to coat.

Pour the oil into a large wok or pot to reach a depth of 3 in (7.5 cm). Heat over moderately high heat until the oil reaches 350°F (175°C) on a deep fry thermometer. Alternatively, you can drop a few bread crumbs into the oil; if the bread crumbs immediately begin to sizzle and brown, the oil is hot enough and ready for frying.

Fry the eggs in the hot oil until golden brown, flipping and turning frequently to ensure even cooking, 5–7 minutes. Transfer the eggs to a large plate lined with paper towels. Season the eggs with salt.

Cut each egg in half lengthwise and serve with Homemade Banana Ketchup (page 24).

SPICY SIZZLING PORK PLATTER SISIG

Sisig is a spicy and citrusy Filipino dish usually comprised of pig ears, snout, and cheeks that have been boiled, grilled, and fried (yes, it's cooked thrice). The whole tasty mess is then served on a hot sizzling skillet. In other words, *sisig* is a platter of sizzling pig's face! And because it is simultaneously spicy, citrusy, smoky, and unapologetically porky, *sisig* is perfect with a cold beer or cocktail—making it the ultimate Filipino bar food. Because pig ears and snout take so long to cook, my quicker version of *sisig* uses only pork jowls. You can usually special-order pork jowls from your butcher, and you can easily order pork jowls online. And if you'd rather not use pork jowls, pork belly is a fine substitute, though I do find the meat in pork jowls to be more tender and succulent. To make this *sisig*, you must first grill the marinated pork in order to render out some of its fat, as well as to achieve wonderfully charred and smoky flavors. I find it's easier to grill the pork when it's cut into long thick slices, like very thick-cut bacon. After grilling, the pork is chopped and then seared in a hot skillet—again to render out more fat, but to also achieve additional crispness. Cooked along with some diced onion and chopped chili pepper, the *sisig* is then ready to be savored and chased down with a cold beverage.

Serves 4–6 as a snack
Prep Time: 30 minutes, plus overnight to marinate
Cooking Time: 40 minutes

½ cup (125 ml) soy sauce
¼ cup (65 ml) white Filipino cane vinegar, or white distilled vinegar
¼ cup (65 ml) fresh *calamansi* juice, or fresh lemon juice
¼ cup (65 ml) *sambal oelek* chili paste
2 cloves garlic, smashed and peeled
2½ lbs (1.25 kg) skinless pork jowl, or skinless pork belly, cut into ½-in (1.25-cm) thick slices
1 large onion, diced
1–2 Thai chili peppers, sliced
2 green onions (scallions), thinly sliced (white and green parts)
Calamansi halves, or lime wedges, for spritzing

Combine the soy sauce, vinegar, calamansi juice (or lemon juice), chili paste, and garlic in a medium bowl. Place the pork into a large resealable food storage bag, and then pour in the marinade and seal the bag. Place the bag in the refrigerator and marinate overnight.

Heat a grill for high-heat, indirect cooking (one side of the grill should be very hot, and the other side cool) and brush the grill grates with oil.

Remove the pork from the marinade and discard the marinade. Place the pork slices on the hot part of the grill and cook, turning every few minutes, until the edges are charred and nicely caramelized, 10–15 minutes. Because of the high fat content in the pork, you may have flare-ups on the grill. In this case, just move the pork to the cool side of the grill until the flames subside.

After the pork has browned directly over the heat, move it to the cool side of the grill and cover the grill. This will allow additional fat to render out of the pork without causing flare-ups over the direct heat. Cook for 10–15

SISIG USA

Because *sisig* is so incredibly delicious, this unlikeliest of Filipino foods has now gone mainstream. If you frequent any Filipino food establishment in the U.S. (from gourmet restaurants, to mom-and-pop shops), chances are that their menus feature some version of *sisig*. During the summer of 2010, I began selling *sisig* from my gourmet Filipino food truck, The Manila Machine. Believe it or not, the people of Los Angeles couldn't get enough and it soon became my best seller. In fact, after enjoying *sisig* from The Manila Machine, many of my customers went the extra step of sporting my infamous (and perhaps now a collector's item) "I Eat Pig Face" t-shirts. Now that's *sisig* love!

SPANISH GARLIC SHRIMP GAMBAS AL AJILO

Although *gambas al ajillo* may be a staple in Spanish *tapas* joints, the same dish has become popular as Filipino *pulutan* as well. Full of garlic flavor with a hint of citrus and spice, while also amazingly simple to prepare, it's easy to see how this dish is a favorite in either country.

Serves 4 as a snack
Prep Time: 5 minutes
Cooking Time: 10 minutes

¼ cup (65 ml) olive oil
6 cloves garlic, minced
½ teaspoon dried red pepper flakes
1 lb (500 g) raw medium-sized shrimp, peeled and deveined
1 tablespoon fresh *calamansi* juice, or fresh lemon juice
½ teaspoon coarse salt, plus more, to taste
½ teaspoon freshly ground black pepper, plus more, to taste
¼ teaspoon smoked Spanish paprika, or regular paprika
3 tablespoons chopped fresh parsley, for garnish

Heat the oil in a large sauté pan over moderately high heat. When the oil begins to shimmer, add the garlic and red pepper flakes and cook until the garlic just begins to brown, 1–2 minutes.

Stir in the rest of the ingredients, except for the parsley, and cook until the shrimp turn pink and are cooked through, 3–4 minutes. Taste the shrimp and season to taste with more salt and pepper if needed.

Transfer the shrimp, along with the rest of the contents in the pan, to a large platter. Serve the shrimp garnished with parsley, and with crusty bread for dipping in the oil and garlic.

minutes more, turning the pork occasionally.

Transfer the pork slices to a cutting board and set aside to cool. When the pork is cool enough to handle, cut it into ¼-in (6-mm) cubes. Heat a large heavy skillet (preferably cast-iron) over high heat. Add the cubed pork, along with the onion and chili pepper, and cook and stir until the onion softens and becomes tender, about 5 minutes.

If needed, pour off fat that has accumulated at the bottom of the pan. Garnish with the green onion and serve the sizzling *sisig* in the hot skillet with *calamansi* or limes for spritzing, and with steamed white rice on the side.

VINTAGE COCKTAILS FROM THE PHILIPPINES

The Philippines have a long alcohol-soaked history with its own collection of indigenous spirits. Among some of these potent drinks are *tuba*, made from fermented palm sap, *lambanog*, made from the fermented sap of coconut trees, *basi*, made from fermented sugarcane juice, and the Filipino rice wine known as *tapuy*. But as Filipino food historian and author Felice Sta. Maria wrote, "The cocktail came with Uncle Sam." It should be of no surprise, then, that if the Americans could make a can of Spam popular in the Philippines, then perhaps bottles of whiskey and gin

would be a much easier sell. As the American presence grew in the Philippines during the early 1900s, so too did various watering holes, bars, and nightclubs. Soon, American-run establishments that catered to American military officers began introducing a variety of mixed concoctions similar (yet exotically different) to those back in the U.S. Before long, these cocktails would move beyond the nightclubs and find their way into the bars of privileged hotels and country clubs across the Philippines that catered to the military elite, visiting dignitaries and foreign adven-

turers. One such adventurer was American author Charles H. Baker Jr. Baker, a gallivanter if there ever was one, traveled across the world seeking the best in food and drink (sweet gig, no?). When he arrived in Manila in 1926, Baker was so impressed by the Filipino mixologists and their potent potables that he included nearly twenty of their cocktails in his book *The Gentleman's Companion, Vol. II*, a book of international cocktails published in 1939. Two of those cocktails—The Gin Fizz Tropical and The Baguio Skin—are included here in the following pages.

CALAMANSI SIMPLE SYRUP

Because granulated sugar can be difficult to completely dissolve in cold liquids and alcohol, simple syrup can be used as a quick and easy way to sweeten many drinks and cocktails. I've found that steeping *calamansi* rinds in the syrup lends the distinct flavor and aroma from the little Filipino citrus fruit. If you don't have *calamansi* limes on hand, you can use the zest from a lemon and an orange, or leave the citrus out entirely for a non-flavored simple syrup.

Makes about 1½ cups (375 ml) of simple syrup.

1 lb (500 g) *calamansi*, washed and stems removed
2 cups (400 g) sugar
1 cup (250 ml) water

Cut each *calamansi* lime in half, and then squeeze the juice through a sieve and into a small container. Set aside the *calamansi* rinds. Discard the seeds in the sieve and save the *calamansi* juice for another use.

Place the reserved rinds, sugar, and water into a saucepan over high heat and bring to a boil while stirring frequently. Reduce the heat to low, and simmer for 10 minutes, stirring until the sugar dissolves. Remove from the heat, and then cover the pot and allow the syrup to cool completely to room temperature.

Pour the syrup through a fine mesh sieve set over a large bowl. Press down on the rinds in the sieve to extract as much liquid as possible. Discard the rinds. Store calamansi syrup in a lidded container and refrigerate for up to a month.

GIN FIZZ TROPICAL

This cocktail is adapted from Charles H. Baker Jr.'s *The Gentleman's Companion, Vol. II*—a tome originally published in 1939, wherein Baker gallivanted to all ends of the earth to imbibe in all sorts of alcoholic beverages. One such beverage was the Gin Fizz Tropical, a drink Baker first encountered in the Philippines. Baker wrote:

> THE GIN FIZZ TROPICAL, Being One More Sound Bit of Liquid Nourishment from where, to Our Routine Mind, Exists the Best & Most Consistent Group of Mixed Drinks—& Mixed Drink Mixers—on Earth: Manila, P.I.

Indeed, after mixing and tasting this refreshingly light and crisp drink for yourself, you'll be in complete agreement with Mr. Baker. The key to any fizz though, including this tropical riff, is to properly incorporate the egg white by shaking the Impyerno (read: hell) out of your cocktail shaker. Fill the shaker as directed and then shake it good and hard for at least 30 seconds without ice, and then another 30 seconds with ice—but a whole minute or more with that ice would be better. And if your arms tire after a half-minute, hand the shaker off to a friend (the recipe can be easily doubled, you know).

Makes 1 drink
Prep time: 5 minutes

2 oz (60 ml) gin
1 oz (30 ml) fresh *calamansi* juice, or fresh lime juice
½ oz (15 ml) Calamansi Simple Syrup (opposite),
   or regular simple syrup
½ oz (15 ml) fresh or canned pineapple juice
1 raw egg white
Ice cubes
Soda water, chilled
Pineapple slice, or lime wheel, for garnish

Combine the gin, *calamansi* juice, *Calamansi* Simple Syrup, pineapple juice, and egg white in a cocktail shaker and shake vigorously for 30 seconds. Add a big handful of ice to the shaker, and then again shake vigorously for at least another 30 seconds.

   Strain into a chilled, empty (no ice) Collins glass and top with chilled soda water. Garnish with the pineapple slice, or lime wheel, and enjoy.

BARTENDER'S NOTE: If you are averse to using a raw egg white in your cocktail, you can substitute a ½ oz (15 ml) of pasteurized egg white for the raw egg white. Pasteurized egg whites are usually sold in small cartons at most grocery stores.

   Alternatively, you can omit the egg white altogether, although the finished drink will lack the wonderful froth and rich mouthfeel that the egg white provides.

THE BAGUIO SKIN COCKTAIL

This is another drink I adapted from Charles H. Baker Jr.'s *The Gentleman's Companion, Vol. II*. Although dead simple to prepare, The Baguio Skin Cocktail is indeed potent. The spicy aroma of fresh nutmeg and a slug of rum keeps the drinker warm—perhaps as an antidote to the cooler climate of Baguio, the mountain city namesake of this drink. Baker wrote of Baguio and the cocktail: "Baguio is the summer, rainy season retreat of civil and military Manila. We found this drink there, 7000 feet up, sitting before an open fire at the Country Club, looking out through the windows while the cloud slowly came down and tucked the 18th fairway under its wing." Fireplaces, country clubs, and golf aren't the first things that come to mind when I think of the Philippines, at least not before drinking a Baguio Skin or two.

Makes 1 drink
Prep Time: 5 minutes

1 teaspoon Calamansi Simple Syrup (page 114), or regular simple syrup
2 dashes orange bitters
Ice cubes
2 oz (60 ml) gold rum
Pinch of freshly grated nutmeg

For the garnish:
Calamansi lime, or a twist of lime peel

Combine the *Calamansi* Simple Syrup and the bitters in an old-fashioned glass. Add enough ice to fill the glass half way, and then stir in the rum. Grate just a pinch of nutmeg over the glass and garnish with the lime. *Mabuhay!*

BARTENDER'S NOTE: Orange bitters (such as Regan's, Fee Brother's, or Angostura Orange) can be found at most well-stocked liquor stores, or it can be ordered from various online retailers.

THE CHIEF LAPU LAPU COCKTAIL

This cocktail is adapted from Jeff Berry's *Beachbum Berry Remixed*—a book that beautifully details a wide variety of vintage Tiki cocktails. The Chief Lapu Lapu is a classic Tiki drink named after the famed Filipino chieftain largely credited with killing Ferdinand Magellan in 1521. Keeping to the Tiki tradition of renaming a drink after it's been tinkered with, I call my version of this cocktail the "Datu Lapu Lapu," wherein *"datu"* is the Filipino word for "chief." With dark and light rums providing the base spirits, this cocktail, like its warrior namesake, has quite the strong kick. Unlike the legendary warrior, the drink also has a refreshingly sweet and sour side as passion fruit syrup and citrus juice lend balance, as well as a sweet and fruity perfume. Hail to the Datu!

Makes 1 drink
Prep Time: 5 minutes

Ice cubes
1½ oz (45 ml) dark Jamaican rum
1½ oz (45 ml) light Puerto Rican rum
2 oz (60 ml) fresh *calamansi* juice, or fresh lemon juice
3 oz (90 ml) fresh orange juice
1 oz (30 ml) Calamansi Simple Syrup (page 114), or regular simple syrup
1 oz (30 ml) passion fruit syrup

For the garnish:
Long strip of orange peel
Calamansi lime (optional)

Combine all of the cocktail ingredients in a cocktail shaker filled with ice and shake vigorously until well chilled, about 30 seconds. Strain into a chilled large snifter glass filled with fresh ice cubes. Garnish with orange peel and *calamansi* lime (if using) and serve with a straw.

> **BARTENDER'S NOTES:** The rich molasses flavor of a good Jamaican dark rum (such as Coruba), and brightness of a good Puerto Rican light rum (such as Don Q Cristal) do wonders in this drink. But any good quality dark and light rum will work just as well.
>
> Passion fruit syrup (by brands such as Torani, Monin, or Trader Vic's) can be found online, or at any well-stocked liquor store. If you can't find passion fruit syrup, grenadine can be substituted, but your drink will lack the distinct flavor and fruitiness imparted by the passion fruit syrup.
>
> If you'd rather have a professional mix a Chief Lapu Lapu for you, head on over to the Tiki-Ti—an old Tiki bar in Los Angeles opened by Filipino-American Ray Buhen in 1961. Today, the Tiki-Ti continues to mix the best Chief Lapu Lapu outside of your home bar.

MANILA-ACAPULCO GROG

The term "grog" historically refers to a mixture of rum, water and citrus juice that was rationed to British sailors beginning in the eighteenth century. The grog was meant to keep sailors content with a daily ration of rum, as well as scurvy-free with the lemon or lime juice squeezed into the drink. In more recent times, however, "grog" refers to any number of Tiki cocktails containing that same combination of rum, water, and citrus juice (e.g. Navy Grog, Coffee Grog, Luau Grog, etc.)—keeping imbibers content, and yes, probably scurvy-free as well.

My present-day interpretation of grog is a drink inspired by the Manila-Acapulco Galleons that traveled between Mexico and the Philippines between 1565–1815. During this 250-year stretch, Spain transported goods between its two colonies, thereby introducing innumerable Mexican influences into Filipino cuisine and vice versa. In fact, there were a number of Filipinos that jumped ship and remained in Mexico, eventually teaching the Mexicans to make Filipino palm wine (*tuba*) from Mexican coconut palms.

My Manila-Acapulco Grog combines Filipino rum, Mexican coffee liqueur, coconut water, and fresh *calamansi* juice (or lime juice)—a modern combination that I'm sure any Filipino, Mexican, or British seafarer would have enjoyed.

Makes 1 drink
Prep Time: 5 minutes

Ice cubes
4 oz (120 ml) coconut water
2 oz (60 ml) rum (such as Tanduay Dark
 or Bacardi Gold)
½ oz (15 ml) coffee liqueur (such as Kahlua)
½ oz (15 ml) fresh *calamansi* juice,
 or fresh lime juice
½ oz (15 ml) *Calamansi* Simple Syrup
 (page 114), or regular simple syrup

For the garnish:
Calamansi lime, or a lime wheel

Combine all of the ingredients in a cocktail shaker filled with ice and shake vigorously until well chilled, about 30 seconds. Strain into a large mug filled with fresh ice cubes. Garnish the drink with a lime wheel or a *calamansi* lime.

> **BARTENDER'S NOTES:** Because of its increasing popularity as a health drink, coconut water can be easily found in most grocery stores, and is often packaged in tetra paks or plastic bottles.
> Filipino rum (Tanduay Dark) can be found in most Asian and Filipino markets. But you can use any good quality dark rum in this drink as well.

THE BLOODY MARIO

My take on the classic bloody Mary uses a variety of potent Filipino flavors: spicy freshly-grated ginger, fiery Filipino vinegar, and a small dose of fish sauce to give this drink some savoriness and saltiness.

The Bloody Mario is named after my dad: Mario Alexander Prieto "Boy" Gapultos. Yes, that's his full name. He's a man of few words, but one who can put away many drinks—a man who might benefit from a hair-of-the-dog-type of drink such as this.

Makes 1 drink
Prep Time: 5 minutes

Ice cubes
2 oz (60 ml) vodka
3 oz (90 ml) chilled tomato juice
½ oz (15 ml) fresh *calamansi* juice, or fresh lemon juice
1 teaspoon spicy vinegar (from Spicy Pickled Peppers—page 20), or other hot sauce (see note)
1 teaspoon fish sauce
1 teaspoon grated fresh ginger
Freshly ground black pepper, to taste

For the garnish:
Cherry tomato
Pickled chili pepper
Bamboo skewer

Combine all of the cocktail ingredients in a cocktail shaker filled with ice and shake vigorously until well chilled, about 30 seconds. Strain into a glass filled with fresh ice cubes. Garnish the drink with the cherry tomato and chili pepper speared onto the bamboo skewer. Serve immediately.

> **BARTENDER'S NOTES:** Like any Bloody Mary recipe, my version is adaptable to suit anyone's particular tastes. Use my recipe as a starting point, and then add more spicy vinegar or fish sauce as needed.
>
> If you don't have a batch of Spicy Pickled Peppers (page 20) already made, you can instead substitute your favorite vinegar-based hot sauce. Sriracha hot sauce also works well in this recipe. For another dimension of flavor, substitute gin for the vodka.
>
> Vuqo, a Filipino coconut vodka available in Asian markets, can be used instead of regular vodka.

CHAPTER 7

DESSERTS AND SWEET SNACKS
MINATAMIS AT MERIENDA

My Grandma Esther is a Jack-of-all-trades, or should I say a Jill-of-all-trades. After earning a degree in Home Economics from the University of the Philippines, she managed to raise six children, teach elementary school in the U.S. for over 20 years, and still found the time to obtain a beautician's license! I'm not sure which childhood memory gives me the most delight: my grandmother baking a multi-tiered, beautifully decorated wedding cake for one of my aunts, or my grandmother giving my older brother a Greg Brady-esque perm. For the sake of this book, I'll go with the cake. Needless to say, my grandmother was just as skilled in making American desserts as she was with traditional Filipino sweets.

My mother, Clarita, is also skilled at making desserts (though, regrettably, her only barbershop skills involved the use of a bowl and a pair of scissors), as she would just as often bake chocolate chip cookies and cheesecakes as she would a sweet Filipino rice cake.

In this section, you will find some of my favorite Filipino sweets (many of which were inspired by my grandmother and mother). From coconut dumplings drizzled with a rum and coconut sauce, to a Bourbon-imbued Filipino candy, and even a coffee and chocolate rice porridge adorned with bacon, these sweet recipes are a mix of old-school and new, just like my grandmother and mother.

MINI MANGO TURNOVERS MANGO EMPANADAS

The small apple hand pies served at a certain fast food chain are a guilty pleasure of mine. That is, they were a guilty pleasure until I discovered a similarly prepared pie at a Filipino fast food chain. But instead of just apples, these little Filipino pies were filled with mangoes and peaches. That's twice the types of fruit for the same amount of guilt! Although I loved these double-filled Filipino pastries, I soon figured out that I can make better pies at home—and for less time and money than spent at the local drive-through window.

When fresh peaches are at their best during the summer months, I do pair them with mangoes in this recipe—using one cup of each fruit. Otherwise, I stick to an all-mango pie, which is just as delicious. And with a touch of fresh lime juice and dark rum, my sweet mango pies are baked in a buttery and flaky crust—still a guilty pleasure for sure, but only when I eat all 12 of these little pastries (which I've been known to do).

Makes 12 empanadas
Prep Time: 25 minutes
Cooking Time: 30 minutes

For the filling:
2 cups (330 g) diced fresh mango (about 2 mangoes), or 1 cup (150 g) each diced fresh mango and diced fresh peaches
¼ teaspoon coarse salt
4 tablespoons brown sugar
1 tablespoon fresh *calamansi* juice, or fresh lime juice
1 tablespoon dark rum
1 teaspoon cornstarch

For the crust:
1 recipe Flaky Pastry Pie Crust (page 23), or 1 store-bought pie crust
1 large egg, beaten

Preheat the oven to 375°F (190°C).

To make the filling, stir together all of the filling ingredients in a medium saucepan over moderately high heat. When the mixture begins to bubble, reduce the heat to low and simmer, stirring occasionally, until the mangoes soften and the liquid thickens into a glaze, 2–3 minutes. Remove from the heat and allow to cool completely.

Meanwhile, if using Flaky Pastry Pie Crust, roll out the dough for the empanadas as shown on page 34. If using store-bought pie crust, cut out 12 rounds of dough that are each 4–5 in (10–13 cm) in diameter.

To fill the empanadas, place a tablespoon of the cooled filling in the center of each disc of prepared dough. Gently fold the circle of dough over the filling to form a half moon. Carefully press the edges of the dough around the filling to get rid of any air pockets, and then gently crimp and seal the edges of the dough with the tines of a fork. Using a sharp knife, cut a 1-in (2.5-cm) vent in the center of each empanada. Brush the top surface of the empanada with the beaten egg, and then place on a baking sheet lined with parchment paper.

Bake the empanadas in the oven until the crust is golden brown, 25–30 minutes. Serve warm.

HOMEMADE MACAPUNO COCONUT ICE CREAM

Peruse the freezer section of any Asian market and you may notice the array of brightly colored and exotic Filipino ice cream flavors on display. With tropical flavors like *ube* (sweet purple yam), *halo-halo* (mixed fruits and sweet beans), avocado, mango, and jackfruit, it's easy to see the Filipino's love of the sweet treat. My favorite variety of Filipino ice cream is *macapuno*, which I've found is simple enough to make at home. If you have an ice cream maker hiding in your cupboard somewhere, you'll want to break it out for this recipe as it features bits of sweet *macapuno* coconut strings (see page 17) embedded in a rich coconut custard.

Makes about 1 quart (1 liter)
Prep Time: 10 minutes, plus overnight to chill in the refrigerator
Cooking Time: 20 minutes, plus 4 hours to freeze in the freezer

1 cup (250 g) jarred *macapuno* coconut strings, or 1 cup (250 g) sweetened shredded coconut
1½ cups (375 ml) canned unsweetened coconut milk
1½ cups (375 ml) heavy cream
½ cup (100 g) sugar
Pinch of salt
4 large egg yolks

Place the *macapuno* in a fine mesh strainer positioned over a small bowl. Drain the *macapuno* for 10–15 minutes and discard any liquid that accumulates in the bowl. Roughly chop the drained *macapuno* into small pieces.

Add the chopped *macapuno*, coconut milk, heavy cream, sugar, and salt to a large saucepan over moderately high heat. Warm and stir the mixture until it just begins to bubble, and then immediately remove the saucepan from the heat.

Whisk the egg yolks in a medium bowl. Slowly add the warmed coconut milk mixture, whisking constantly, to the egg yolks. If too much hot liquid is added to the egg yolks too quickly, the egg yolks will curdle and scramble. So be sure to add the warmed milk ladleful by ladleful as you whisk. Once all of the warmed milk mixture has been added to the eggs, pour everything back into the saucepan.

Return the saucepan to medium heat and cook, stirring and scraping the bottom of the pan constantly, until the mixture thickens and coats the back of a spoon, or until the mixture

reaches 170°F (77°C) on an instant-read thermometer.

Pour the custard mixture into a clean medium bowl set over an ice bath and stir until cool. Cover the custard mixture and place it in the refrigerator overnight until thoroughly chilled.

Once the custard is completely chilled,

freeze it in an ice cream maker according to the manufacturer's instructions.

> **COOK'S NOTE:** For an extra layer of flavor, drizzle some Rum and Coconut Caramel Sauce (page 125), and the tiniest sprinkling of sea salt, over the ice cream when serving.

SWEET CORN AND COCONUT PANNA COTTA MAJA BLANCA

Literally translated, *maja blanca* means "white lady" and refers to the creamy white consistency of this sweet coconut pudding. Although the pudding is usually thickened with cornstarch, I prefer using powdered gelatin as it yields a smoother and creamier consistency.

The use of sweet corn in a dessert is not unusual in the Philippines. In this case, the corn adds sweetness as well as texture to the *panna cotta*. If fresh sweet corn isn't in season or unavailable, you can opt to use 1 cup (250 g) of frozen corn kernels instead, or omit the corn altogether for a completely smooth *panna cotta*.

Serves 6
Prep Time: 10 minutes, plus overnight to set up
Cooking Time: 30 minutes

1 cup (250 g) fresh sweet white corn kernels (from about 1 large ear), or 1 cup (250 g) frozen corn kernels
2 cups (500 ml) canned unsweetened coconut milk
1 cup (250 ml) heavy cream
½ cup (100 g) sugar
1 teaspoon vanilla extract
3 tablespoons cold water
2½ teaspoons unflavored gelatin powder
½ cup (20 g) sweetened shredded coconut

Combine the corn kernels, coconut milk, cream, and sugar in a large saucepan over medium heat. Stir until the sugar dissolves and the mixture just begins to bubble. Remove from heat and stir in the vanilla extract.

Pour the cold water into a large bowl, and then sprinkle the gelatin over the water and let stand for 5 minutes. Pour the warm coconut milk mixture over the gelatin and stir until the gelatin is completely dissolved.

Evenly divide the *panna cotta* mixture between six ramekins or glasses. Cover each *panna cotta* with plastic wrap and chill in the refrigerator overnight until completely firm.

Preheat the oven to 325°F (160°C)

Spread the shredded coconut into an even layer on a baking sheet. Place the coconut in the oven and toast until golden brown, stirring once, 8–10 minutes.

Remove the *panna cotta* from the refrigerator and uncover. Serve each *panna cotta* garnished with the toasted coconut.

SILKEN TOFU, TAPIOCA AND CARAMEL PARFAIT TAHO

On my last trip to the Philippines, I encountered a street vendor carrying a long wooden pole across his shoulders. At either end of the pole was a metal bucket—one bucket held tapioca pearls and a caramel sauce in separate compartments, and the other bucket contained warm and soft silken tofu. The vendor then scooped some tofu into a plastic cup, layered in some tapioca, and then topped it all off with a drizzle of caramel sauce. While cold tofu may seem out of place in a warm dessert, it is the perfect blank canvas for a sweet caramel sauce—especially my Rum and Coconut Caramel Sauce. And with chewy tapioca pearls to contrast the smooth and creamy tofu, this is a sweet dessert layered with incredible flavors and textures.

Serves 4
Prep Time: 10 minutes
Cooking Time: 15 minutes

1 cup (170 g) large dried tapioca pearls
12 oz (350 g) silken tofu
1 recipe Rum and Coconut Caramel Sauce

Cook the tapioca pearls according to the package instructions. Drain and set the cooked tapioca aside.

Layer spoonfuls of the tofu in the bottom of small bowls or dessert cups, and then add a few spoonfuls of the cooked tapioca followed by a drizzle of the caramel sauce. Continuing layering the ingredients to fill the bowls or cups, and serve immediately.

RUM AND COCONUT CARAMEL SAUCE

Makes about ¾ cup (185 ml)
Prep Time: 5 minutes
Cooking Time: 15 minutes

½ cup (90 g) brown sugar
1 tablespoon water
½ cup (125 ml) coconut milk
1 tablespoon dark rum
Pinch of sea salt

Place the sugar and water in a large heavy-bottomed saucepan over medium heat. Once the sugar completely melts and begins to darken, stir constantly until the mixture begins to bubble and thicken, 2–3 minutes.

Slowly whisk in the coconut milk—the mixture will bubble furiously, so take care not to burn yourself. Continue stirring the mixture over medium heat until it is thoroughly combined and begins to thicken into a caramel, 3–5 minutes more.

Remove the sauce from the heat. Stir in the rum and salt. Whisk to combine.

COOK'S NOTES: Store the caramel in a plastic squeeze bottle for up to a month in the refrigerator for easy drizzling and dispensing.
Reheat cold caramel with 10-second intervals in the microwave, as needed.

BOURBON BUTTERED PECAN CRUMBLES POLVORON

Polvoron are festive sweet treats that are not unlike very fragile and crumbly shortbread cookies. Which is fitting, considering that the Spanish word *"polvo"* translates to "powder."

In its most basic form, *polvoron* consist of toasted flour, sugar, powdered milk, and butter—but in the Philippines, flavor variations run the gamut from cookies and cream to chocolate chip. In my opinion though, toasted pecans glazed in butter and bourbon elevate the candy to another level.

Fancy ingredients aside, toasted flour is the key to a great *polvoron*. Gently heating the flour in a dry pan lends a wonderfully nutty and toasted flavor to the finished candies, which are then individually wrapped in brightly colored cellophane or tissue paper. Though not as colorful, but just as festive, regular aluminum foil can also be used to wrap the candies "bon-bon-style."

As a child, and even today, I would unwrap one end of the *polvoron* wrapper and funnel the powdered candy into my mouth. *Polvoron*—crumbles in your mouth, not in your hand.

> **COOK'S NOTE:** The small amount of alcohol in the bourbon burns away from the heat in the pan, so you can serve these candies to children. But if you'd rather not use liquor at all, the bourbon can be omitted completely.

Makes 15–18 candies
Prep Time: 5 minutes
Cooking Time: 30 minutes

½ cup (70 g) all-purpose flour
¼ cup (20 g) powdered milk
¼ cup (50 g) sugar
¼ cup (25 g) coarsely chopped pecans
6 tablespoons butter, cut into small pieces
2 tablespoons bourbon whiskey (optional)
Pinch of salt
Colored cellophane, tissue paper, or tin foil,
 for wrapping candies

Toast the flour in a large, dry non-stick pan over moderately high heat. Constantly shake the pan and stir the flour until the flour just begins to turn blonde or a very light nutty brown, 5–10 minutes. Don't be alarmed if the flour begins to smoke. If this happens, remove the pan from the heat and continue to stir constantly until the smoking subsides, and then return the pan to the heat and continue to toast the flour until it changes color and smells of roasted nuts.

Once the flour is toasted, immediately transfer it to a large bowl. Whisk in the powdered milk and sugar, and stir until well combined. Set the flour mixture aside.

Wipe out the pan with a paper towel to ensure that no flour was left behind. Return the pan to moderately high heat and add the pecans. Stir the pecans until they just begin to toast and start to smell nutty, 2–3 minutes. Remove from the heat and add the butter, bourbon (if using), and salt, and stir until the butter is completely melted.

Add the melted butter and pecan mixture to the flour mixture and stir until well combined and the mixture resembles wet sand. Place in the refrigerator for 10 minutes—this rest in the refrigerator helps to make the candy easier to mold and shape.

Shape the candies by tightly packing some of the mixture into a tablespoon measure. Gently invert and tap the tablespoon onto a cookie sheet lined with parchment paper to release the molded candy. Repeat until all of the mixture has been formed into candies. Place the cookie sheet into the refrigerator for another 10 minutes to set the candy.

Serve immediately, or individually wrap each candy in a square of cellophane, tissue paper, or foil, and store in the refrigerator. For a more crumbly texture, serve the candies at room temperature.

CANDY CRUMBLES

A special spring-loaded candy mold is usually needed to shape *polvoron*, but these molds can be difficult to find even at Filipino markets. Even better than a traditional *polvoron* mold is a small, spring-loaded cookie dough/ice cream scoop with a 1-tablespoon capacity—the kind with the metal arm that sweeps and ejects food from the scoop.

But even without fancy spring-loaded tools, I've figured out that if you firmly press the *polvoron* mixture into the bowl of a regular tablespoon measure, a gentle tap is all that is needed to unmold the candy. Once the candy is formed, it can be firmed up in the refrigerator and then parceled into your choice of wrapping paper.

CRUNCHY SWEET BANANA NUT ROLLS TURON

Turon are deep-fried banana-filled spring rolls smothered in a caramel candy coating. A quick fry in hot oil renders a creamy and custardy texture from the bananas, while the *lumpia* wrapper becomes crispy and crunchy. Inspired by the terrific banana nut muffins that my wife sometimes makes for breakfast, I decided to transfer these same flavors over to this Filipino dessert. With chopped pecans and brown sugar sprinkled on the inside, as well as on the outside, of the spring rolls, these *turon* are transformed with the classic flavors and crunch of bananas and nuts.

Makes 12 rolls
Prep Time: 30 minutes
Cooking Time: 15 minutes

2 tablespoons chopped pecans
2 tablespoons brown sugar
3 large ripe-but-firm bananas
8 square spring roll wrappers (8 x 8 in/20 x 20 cm)
Water, for sealing the wrappers
High-heat oil, for frying

Mix together the pecans and brown sugar in a small bowl and set aside.

Peel the bananas, and then cut each banana in half crosswise, and then in half again lengthwise to yield 12 slices of banana total.

Turon are filled and rolled in the same fashion as *lumpia*. Follow the illustrated instructions to the right for more information on how to fill and roll the *turon*.

To fry the *turon*, fill a large frying pan with at least a ½ in (1.25 cm) of canola oil. Heat over moderately high heat until the oil reaches 350°F (175°C) on a deep fry thermometer. Alternatively, you can drop a small piece of spring roll wrapper into the oil, if it begins to immediately brown and sizzle, the oil is ready.

When the oil is ready, fry the *turon* in batches, being careful to not overcrowd the pan. Fry the rolls, turning occasionally, until golden and crisp, 3–4 minutes total. If frying frozen *turon*, add 1 minute of cooking time to each side. Transfer the fried *turon* to a paper towel-lined plate to drain. Continue frying until all *turon* are golden brown.

While the *turon* are still hot, sprinkle any of the remaining pecan and brown sugar mixture over the top of the spring rolls.

Serve the *turon* immediately.

> **COOK'S NOTE:** Before frying, you can roll the *turon* ahead of time and freeze them for future use. To freeze *turon*, place them in a single layer on a baking sheet and place in the freezer until completely frozen. You can fry the *turon* directly out of the freezer as directed above.

HOW TO ROLL THE TURON

1. Place 1 spring roll wrapper on a clean, dry work surface so that one corner of the wrapper is pointing at you (positioned like a diamond, rather than a square). Place one banana slice horizontally across the spring roll wrapper, just below the center of the wrapper.

2. Sprinkle just 1 teaspoon of the pecan and brown sugar mixture over the banana slice—do not overfill the spring roll or the pecans will puncture the wrapper.

3. Take the corner closest to you and roll it up over the filling.

4. Fold the left and right corners of the wrapper over the filling. Using your fingers, or a pastry brush, dab the edges of the wrapper with water to ensure a good seal.

5. Continue to roll the spring roll toward the final corner at the top. Place the finished spring roll seam-side down, underneath a moist paper towel, and continue rolling the rest of the spring rolls. Reserve any of the remaining pecan and brown sugar mixture to sprinkle atop of the fried *turon* before serving.

CRISPY SWEET POTATO AND SESAME SEED DUMPLINGS BUCHI

Filipino *buchi* are nearly identical to the popular Chinese *dim sum* staple of crispy and sweet sesame balls, also known as *ma tuan* or *jin deui*. The most common versions of these dumplings, both Chinese and Filipino, feature a chewy rice flour dough covered in sesame seeds and filled with sweet red bean paste. These dumplings are so popular in the Philippines that they are even served at Filipino fast food chains. My grandmother's homemade *buchi*, however, lacks the bean paste filling altogether. She instead mixes mashed sweet potato right into her rice flour dough. In the United States, yellow-fleshed tubers are generally labeled as "sweet potatoes" and orange-fleshed tubers are generally labeled as "yams," though either can be used in this recipe. I prefer the orange-fleshed yams because it is what my grandmother uses, and also because the color is more vibrant in the finished product. The resultant sesame ball is subtly sweet with a bright orange chewy interior and crispy exterior. My son, Bruce, absolutely loves his great grandmother's sesame dumplings. So whenever we visit my grandmother, she is sure to have a batch of *buchi* already waiting for Bruce.

Makes about 2 dozen dumplings
Prep Time: 45 minutes
Cooking Time: 1 hour, plus 25 minutes for frying

- 1–2 yams (or sweet potatoes), about 1 lb (500 g)
- 2 cups (200 g) glutinous rice flour
- 1 cup (100 g) rice flour
- 1 cup (200 g) sugar
- 1 teaspoon baking powder
- 1–4 tablespoons water, if needed
- ⅓ cup (50 g) raw white sesame seeds
- Oil, for frying

Pre-heat the oven to 400°F (200°C).

Pierce the yam(s)—or sweet potato(es)— several times with the tines of a fork, and then wrap the yam in aluminum foil. Place the yam on the middle rack of the oven and bake until it is completely soft throughout, 45–60 minutes. Remove the yam from the oven set aside until cool enough to handle. Alternatively, you can peel and cut the yam into small chunks and boil in water until soft. Boiling saves time, but roasting better concentrates the flavors and sweetness of the yam.

Add the glutinous rice flour, the rice flour, sugar, and baking powder to a large bowl and whisk well to combine. Cut the softened yam in half lengthwise, and then scoop the flesh of the yam into a separate medium bowl. Discard the yam skins. Using a wooden spoon or potato masher, mash the yam until smooth. You should have just about 2 cups of mashed yam. Add the mashed yam into the flour mixture and mix with your hands until the yam is well combined with the dry ingredients and an orange dough is formed.

Depending on how much moisture is in the yam, you may be able to form a dough without having to add any of the water. The dough should be able to hold its shape and be slightly sticky, but not overly wet. If you find that more liquid is needed to form a dough, add the water a tablespoon at a time until the dough comes together.

Pinch off about a tablespoon of dough and roll it between your palms to form a sphere roughly the size of a golf ball. Place the ball on large platter and cover with plastic wrap to prevent drying. Continue rolling balls from the remaining dough to yield 24–30 balls total.

Pour the sesame seeds into a large bowl. Roll the balls of dough in the sesame seeds until each ball is completely covered, and then place each ball back onto the platter. Roll each sesame seed-covered ball between your hands again to ensure that the sesame seeds stick to the dough.

Pour the oil into a large wok or deep pot to reach a depth of 3 in (7.5 cm). Heat over moderately high heat until the oil reaches 350°F (175°C) on a deep fry thermometer. Alternatively, you can drop a small piece of dough into the hot oil; if it immediately begins to sizzle and brown, the oil is hot enough and ready for frying.

Carefully drop 5–6 dumplings into the hot oil, gently flipping and stirring them to ensure they don't stick together and that they brown evenly. Fry the dumplings until golden brown, 5–7 minutes. If the dumplings brown too quickly on the outside, the center may remain uncooked. So be sure to maintain the heat so that each dumpling fries for 5–7 minutes, or that the oil temperature remains around 350°F (175°C).

Remove the dumplings from the oil and place on a baking sheet lined with paper towels. Repeat until all the dumplings are fried.

Serve warm.

CASSAVA CAKE BIBINGKANG CASSAVA

The term "*bibingka*" usually refers to a certain variety of sweet Filipino cakes made from rice flour, though *cassava* (*yucca*) root can also be used to make a sweet and rich *bibingka* as well. In the United States, fresh *cassava* root can easily be found in Asian and Latin markets, and sometimes in larger grocery stores. However, to save time and effort I do prefer to use frozen grated *cassava* found in Asian markets. Don't be alarmed by the absence of flour in this cake recipe. Because of the high starch content in *cassava*, it alone will be able to absorb the liquid and transform into a sweet and soft cake that may be the easiest dessert you'll ever make.

Makes one 8 x 8-in (20 x 20-cm) cake
Prep Time: 10 minutes
Cooking Time: 1 hour, 15 minutes

For the cake:
4 egg yolks, beaten
One 1-lb (500-g) package frozen grated *cassava*, thawed
1 cup (250 g) jarred *macapuno* coconut strings, or sweetened shredded coconut
1½ cups (375 ml) canned unsweetened coconut milk
½ cup (125 ml) sweetened condensed milk

For the topping:
4 egg whites
¼ cup (65 ml) sweetened condensed milk

Preheat the oven to 350°F (175°C).

To make the cake, combine the egg yolks, *cassava*, *macapuno* (or shredded coconut, if using), coconut milk and the ½ cup (125 ml) sweetened condensed milk in a large bowl and mix well.

Pour the cake batter into a greased 8 x 8-in (20 x 20-cm) cake pan. The cake batter will appear to be very loose and wet at this point, but don't worry, the cassava will absorb most of the liquid during baking. Place the cake pan into the oven and bake until the top of the cake appears dry and no liquid is floating on the surface, 45–60 minutes.

Meanwhile, to make the topping, whisk together the egg whites and the ¼ cup (65 ml) sweetened condensed milk in a medium bowl until very well incorporated. Although you are using egg whites, don't be concerned with making a foam or a meringue, just mix until combined.

Remove the cake from the oven and evenly pour the topping onto the cake. Return the cake to the oven and bake until the topping sets, about 10 minutes more.

Remove the cake from the oven and rest the cake in its pan on a cooling rack. Cool the cake completely before cutting it into squares. The cassava cake can be served at room temperature, or cold out of the refrigerator.

SWEET COCONUT RICE SQUARES BIKO

The term "*suman*" usually refers to sweet desserts or snacks that are individually wrapped and steamed in banana or coconut leaves. The banana or coconut leaf not only makes for a great cooking vessel and transportable package, but it also imbues a fragrant grassy aroma to whatever is held inside. The contents of *suman* can range from sweet rice, cassava root, or even sweet potatoes and bananas.

Biko, on the other hand, is perhaps a streamlined version of *suman* in that sweet rice is first cooked in coconut milk, and then pressed into a cake pan and finished in the oven. My great aunties and mother all made *biko* in this fashion, skipping the often time-consuming practice of wrapping single servings of sweet rice in banana leaves. As a child though, I simply called this dessert "rice cake."

The following recipe is for *biko* cooked in a cake pan and topped with a sweet brown sugar and coconut milk glaze, the way my mother makes it. And to obtain the same sweet fragrance of *suman* wrapped in banana leaves, the cake pan can also be lined with banana leaves.

Makes one 8 x 8-in (20 x 20-cm) cake
Prep Time: 10 minutes
Cooking Time: 1 hour, 30 minutes

For the cake:
Banana leaves (optional), for lining pan
2 cups (500 ml) canned unsweetened coconut milk
2 cups (500 ml) water
¾ cup (175 g) brown sugar
2 cups (450 g) uncooked sweet sticky rice (*malagkit*)
½ teaspoon salt

For the topping:
½ cup (125 ml) canned unsweetened coconut milk
4 tablespoons brown sugar

Preheat the oven to 350°F (175°C).

Line an 8 x 8-in (20 x 20-cm) cake pan with a double layer of banana leaves to ensure that all sides on the inside of the pan are covered. Alternatively, you can grease the pan with nonstick cooking spray. Set the pan aside.

To make the cake, whisk together the 2 cups (500 ml) of coconut milk with the water and ¾ cup (175 g) of brown sugar in a medium saucepan. Stir in the rice and the salt and bring everything to a boil over high heat. Cover the saucepan, reduce the heat to low and simmer, stirring occasionally, until the rice has absorbed most of the liquid, 20–25 minutes. At this stage, the mixture will resemble a thick *risotto* and the rice grains will only be partially cooked. Remove the mixture from the heat. Transfer the rice mixture to the prepared baking pan and spread it into an even layer with a spatula. Set the baking pan aside.

To make the topping, combine the remaining ½ cup (125 ml) of coconut milk with the remaining 4 tablespoons of brown sugar in a small bowl and mix well. Evenly pour the topping over the rice mixture, and then bake the cake in the oven until the topping has set and is brown and caramelized, 35–40 minutes. Remove the cake from the oven and allow to cool completely before cutting into squares.

COOK'S NOTE: Glutinous rice is available in Asian markets labeled as "sweet rice," "sticky rice," or with the Filipino term "*malagkit*." Sweet sticky rice is usually white, but there are also purple or violet varieties to try.

SWEET COCONUT DUMPLINGS WITH RUM AND COCONUT CARAMEL CASCARONE

Cascarone (also known as *bitsu-bitsu* or *bichu-bichu* in various parts of the Philippines) are sweet deep-fried dumplings made from rice flour and coconut milk. Although *cascarone* are normally completely coated in caramel, I find that this causes their crispy exterior to get soggy and wet. So I actually prefer drizzling the caramel over the crisp dumplings, rather than coating them entirely. In this way the dumplings retain their wonderfully crunchy shells with a chewy interior. Traditionally, the *cascarone*'s caramel coating is made from a simple mix of water and sugar, but a quick drizzle of Rum and Coconut Caramel Sauce makes an already great dessert even better.

Makes about 15–20 dumplings
Prep Time: 30 minutes
Cooking Time: 30 minutes

1 cup (100 g) glutinous rice flour
1 cup (100 g) rice flour
½ cup (115 g) jarred *macapuno*,
  chopped, or ½ cup (115 g) sweetened
  shredded coconut
1 cup (250 ml) canned unsweetened
  coconut milk, divided
Oil, for frying
1 recipe Rum and Coconut Caramel
  Sauce (page 125)

Whisk the glutinous rice flour and the rice flour together in a large bowl. Add the *macapuno* (or dried coconut, if using) and half of the coconut milk and stir to combine. Slowly add the rest of the coconut milk, little by little, and continue to mix until a dough comes together. You may not have to use all of the coconut milk. The dough should hold its shape and be slightly sticky, but not overly wet. If you're using dried shredded coconut, more coconut milk may be needed to form the dough.

Pinch off about a tablespoon of dough and roll it between your palms to form a sphere roughly the size of a golf ball. Place the ball on a large platter and cover with plastic wrap to prevent drying. Continue rolling balls from the remaining dough to yield 15–20 balls total.

In a large wok, or a deep pot, pour in the oil to reach a depth of 3 in (7.5 cm). Heat over moderately high heat until the oil reaches 350°F (175°C) on a deep fry thermometer.

Alternatively, you can drop a small pea-sized piece of the dough into the oil—if it immediately begins to sizzle and brown, the oil is hot enough and ready for frying.

Carefully drop 5–6 balls into the hot oil, gently flipping and stirring the balls to ensure that they don't stick together and that they brown evenly. Fry the balls until golden brown, 5–7 minutes. If the dumplings brown too quickly on the outside, the center may remain uncooked. So be sure to maintain the heat so that each dumpling fries for 5–7 minutes, or that the oil temperature remains around 350°F (175°C).

Remove the dumplings from the oil and place on a baking sheet lined with paper towels. Repeat until all the dumplings are fried.

While the dumplings are still warm, place them on a platter and drizzle them with the Rum and Coconut Caramel Sauce. Serve immediately.

TAPIOCA PEARLS WITH COCONUT MILK AND MANGO
TAMBO-TAMBO

When I was a child, it was a rare occasion that I would help out in the kitchen—I was usually busy with things like escaping and/or applying headlocks (I grew up with brothers). But every now and then, I'd lend a hand—especially if it meant I'd get to use my hands to roll rice dough for my favorite comfort dessert. *Tambo-tambo* (also known as *bilo-bilo*) is a warm, sweet porridge of soft tapioca and rice balls simmered in coconut milk. Although the *tambo-tambo* of my childhood was also simmered with things like sweet potatoes, *saba* bananas, and jackfruit, my new recipe is incredibly easy to make with just a simple addition of sweet fresh mangoes in lieu of the traditional starchy root vegetables and fruits. Be sure to use small pearl tapioca for this recipe to contrast to the larger rice balls. Tapioca can be found in most grocery stores, but it is often less expensive in Asian markets.

Serves 4–6
Prep Time: 30 minutes
Cooking Time: 15 minutes

For the tapioca:
½ cup (75 g) small dried tapioca pearls
1 cup (250 ml) water

For the rice flour balls:
1 cup (150 g) glutinous rice flour
½ cup (125 ml) water, plus more as needed

For the porridge:
1¾ cup (400 ml) unsweetened coconut milk
½ cup (125 ml) water
¼ teaspoon salt
½ cup (100 g) sugar
2 ripe mangoes, peeled, deseeded and diced

Soak the tapioca in the 1 cup (250 ml) of water in a small bowl for 30 minutes.

While the tapioca is soaking, make the rice balls. Combine the rice flour with the ½ cup (125 ml) of water in a large bowl and mix until a dough comes together. The dough should be slightly tacky and you should be able to form the dough into a large sphere. If the dough is too dry and crumbly, slowly add more water, one tablespoon at a time, until the dough can hold its shape.

Form the rice flour balls by pinching off about a teaspoon of the dough and rolling it between your palms to form a small sphere about ½ in (1.25 cm) in diameter. You should be able to make about 20 small rice balls from the dough. Cover the rice balls with a damp paper towel and set aside.

Drain the tapioca in a fine-mesh sieve set over the sink and rinse with cold running water. Allow the tapioca to continue draining over the sink.

To make the porridge, combine the coconut milk with the remaining ½ cup (125 ml) of water in a large saucepan. Stir in the salt and the sugar and bring the mixture to a boil over high heat. Reduce the heat to low, and then add the rice balls to the saucepan and gently simmer, stirring to ensure the rice balls don't stick to each other. Continue simmering the rice balls until they are cooked through and become pleasantly chewy, 3–5 minutes. As the rice balls simmer, they will become firmer and expand slightly.

Increase the heat to high and return the liquid to a boil. As soon as the liquid boils, turn off the heat and stir in the drained tapioca pearls. Continue to stir until the tapioca becomes tender and translucent, 2–3 minutes. If the porridge becomes too thick for your liking, you can thin it out with more water or coconut milk.

Stir in the mangoes and serve the porridge warm.

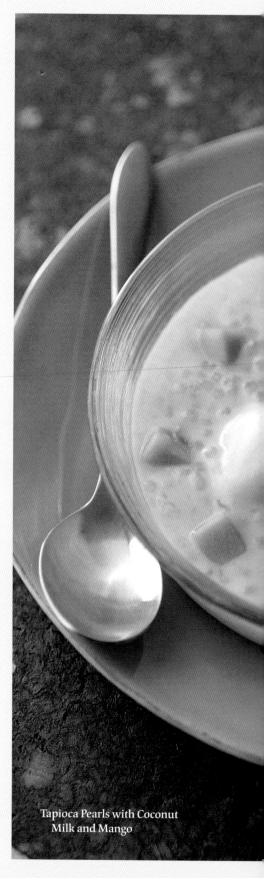

Tapioca Pearls with Coconut Milk and Mango

CHOCOLATE AND COFFEE RICE PUDDING CHAMPORADO

Believe it or not, Filipinos actually eat this chocolate rice pudding for breakfast. And as a savory counterpoint to the sweet chocolate, dried salted fish is traditionally served alongside a bowl of *champorado*. Now that's what I call a hearty breakfast! While *champorado* is usually made with canned evaporated milk and Filipino chocolate tablets, my version is prepared with fresh milk, semi-sweet chocolate chips, coffee and a splash of coffee liqueur. And as a substitute for the traditional side of dried salted fish, I like to sprinkle crisp bacon bits onto my *champorado*. Coffee and bacon in *champorado*? Well, it *is* breakfast after all. And of course, *champorado* makes for an excellent dessert as well.

Serves 4–6
Prep Time: 5 minutes
Cooking Time: 45 minutes

¾ cup (150 g) uncooked sweet sticky rice (*malagkit*)
3 cups (750 ml) milk
1 cup (250 ml) strongly brewed coffee
⅓ cup (75 g) sugar
Pinch of salt
1 cup (250 g) semi-sweet chocolate chips
2 tablespoons coffee liqueur (optional)
2–3 strips of bacon, chopped fine (optional)

Combine the rice, milk, coffee, sugar, and salt in a large saucepan over high heat. While stirring frequently, bring everything to a boil. Reduce the heat to moderately low heat and simmer, stirring frequently, until the rice is tender and the mixture thickens, 30–40 minutes.

Meanwhile, if using, cook the bacon in a small frying pan over medium heat until brown and crisp, 5–7 minutes. Drain the bacon on a plate lined with paper towels and set aside.

Remove the rice mixture from the heat. Add the chocolate chips and stir until they are melted and thoroughly incorporated into the rice. Stir in the coffee liqueur, if using.

Spoon the pudding into individual bowls and serve warm, garnished with the bacon bits (if using).

Alternatively, the *champorado* can be served cold. As such, cover the pudding and store it in the refrigerator until ready to serve. The *champorado* will further thicken in the refrigerator, so if a creamier consistency is desired, it can be thinned out with more milk before being served cold.

MOCHA CHIFFON CUPCAKES WITH BUTTERCREAM FROSTING

Chiffon cake, a light and airy dessert created by an American insurance salesman, may seem like a strange entry in a Filipino cookbook. But walk into most any Filipino bakery and you are just as likely to find a display of brightly decorated chiffon cakes as you are to see native Filipino pastries. Because of America's strong cultural and culinary influence on the Philippines, chiffon cake is very much a part of the Filipino dessert repertoire. Big chain Filipino bakeries, as well as smaller mom-and-pop shops, all crank out various frosted and iced chiffons ranging in tropical flavors from mango, to *pandan*, to *ube* (sweet purple yam). And because instant coffee also became a widely used American ingredient in the Filipino pantry, mocha is another popular variant of chiffon cake. My rendition of mocha chiffon is in cupcake form. Although it may seem like a lot of steps, the procedure for these moist and delicate cupcakes are straightforward and simple. Whipped egg whites provide the airy texture, and chocolate, coffee and coffee liqueur all combine for a sweet mocha flavor.

Makes 24 cupcakes
Prep Time: 20 minutes
Cooking Time: 30 minutes

For the cupcakes:
¾ cup (85 g) cake flour
4 tablespoons unsweetened cocoa
  powder
1½ teaspoons baking powder
¼ teaspoon salt
4 large eggs, separated (4 egg yolks,
  4 egg whites)
⅔ cup (130 g) granulated sugar,
  plus 2 tablespoons
⅓ cup (80 ml) strongly brewed coffee,
  cooled
2 teaspoons coffee liqueur (such as
  Kahlua)
¼ cup (60 ml) vegetable oil
½ teaspoon cream of tartar

For the buttercream:
2½ cups (285 g) powdered sugar
2 tablespoons unsweetened cocoa
  powder
8 tablespoons (1 stick) butter, softened
2 tablespoons strongly brewed coffee,
  cooled
1 tablespoon coffee liqueur (such as
  Kahlua)
Chocolate covered coffee beans,
  for garnish (optional)

Preheat the oven to 325°F (160°C). Prepare muffin tins by lining them with cupcake wrappers and set aside.

To make the cupcakes, sift together the cake flour, cocoa powder, baking powder and salt in a large bowl and whisk until thoroughly combined.

In a medium bowl, beat together the 4 egg yolks and the ⅔ cup (130 g) granulated sugar until the yolks lighten in color and the sugar is completely incorporated. You can use a whisk or an electric hand mixer for this. Add the cooled coffee, coffee liqueur and vegetable oil to the egg mixture and mix until well incorporated. Pour the wet ingredients into the large bowl with the dry ingredients and mix together to form a batter. Set the batter aside.

In the bowl of an electric stand mixer fitted with a whisk, or in a separate clean, large bowl using a hand mixer with clean beaters, whisk the 4 egg whites with the cream of tartar until frothy. While mixing on medium speed, slowly sprinkle in the remaining 2 tablespoons of granulated sugar. Continue to beat the egg whites until they form stiff peaks when the beater is lifted from the bowl, 2–3 minutes.

Gently transfer about one-third of the egg whites into the bowl with the cake batter. Using a spatula, gently fold the egg whites into the batter until just combined, being careful to not deflate the egg whites, as their consistency is a crucial contribution to the airy texture of the final cake. Add another third of the egg whites to the batter and again gently fold until just combined. Gingerly add the last third of the egg whites and gently fold them into the batter.

Evenly divide the cupcake batter into the prepared muffin tins, filling each cup about two-thirds full. Bake the cupcakes in the oven until they are nicely puffed and a toothpick inserted into the middle of a cupcake comes out clean, 12–18 minutes. Remove the cupcakes from the oven and cool completely before frosting.

While the cupcakes are cooling make the buttercream. Sift together the powdered sugar and cocoa powder in a medium bowl and whisk until thoroughly combined.

In the bowl of an electric stand mixer fitted with a paddle attachment, or in a large bowl using a hand mixer, add the butter with the powdered sugar and cocoa mixture and mix on medium speed until thoroughly combined, 2–3 minutes. It may initially seem that there is not enough butter for the dry ingredients, but continue mixing and they will eventually come together to form a cream. Once the butter, powdered sugar and cocoa are completely incorporated, add the coffee and coffee liqueur, and mix until thoroughly combined. Frost the cupcakes with the buttercream and garnish with the chocolate covered coffee beans, if using.

Serves 6
Prep Time: 15 minutes, plus at least 2 hours to chill
Cooking Time: 1 hour

½ cup (100 g) sugar
2 tablespoons water
2 large eggs
4 large egg yolks
One 14-oz (400-ml) can sweetened condensed milk
One 12-oz (350-ml) can evaporated milk
¼ teaspoon salt
1 teaspoon vanilla extract
1 teaspoon grated lemon zest

Set six 6–8-oz (185–250-ml) oven-safe ramekins in a large roasting pan or deep baking dish. Pour enough water into the pan to come halfway up the sides of the ramekins. Remove the ramekins from the pan and set them aside next to the stovetop. Place the pan full of water onto a center rack in the oven and preheat the oven to 325°F (160°C).

Heat the sugar and water in a small saucepan over moderately high heat and bring to a boil. As the sugar boils, carefully and gently swirl the pan. Continue to boil until the sugar takes on a blonde or light brown color, 3–5 minutes—the darker the sugar gets, the more difficult it may be to later remove the *flan* from the ramekins. If the sugar becomes too foamy to judge its color, remove it from the heat until the bubbles subside.

Once the sugar caramelizes and reaches a blonde or light brown color, remove it from the heat and quickly, but very carefully, pour it into each of the ramekins. The caramel will be extremely hot and dangerous, so be careful to not burn yourself when pouring it into the ramekins. Quickly tilt the ramekins to ensure that the bottom surfaces are evenly coated in the caramel. Set the ramekins aside and allow the caramel to cool and harden into a candy.

Meanwhile, beat together the eggs and egg yolks in a large bowl. Stir in the sweetened condensed milk, evaporated milk, salt, and vanilla extract, and whisk until thoroughly combined. Pour the custard mixture through a fine-mesh sieve set over another large bowl—this will help to ensure a smoother *flan* by straining out any bubbles or un-whisked egg proteins. After straining the custard mixture, gently stir in the lemon zest.

Evenly distribute the custard mixture into each of the ramekins. Carefully place the ramekins into the water bath in the oven and bake for 30–45 minutes, or until the custard is set, but still jiggles slightly in the center when shaken. Note that *flans* in wide, shallow ramekins tend to bake more quickly than those in narrow and deep ramekins. Remove the *flans* from the water bath in the oven and set them aside to cool to room temperature. Wrap each of the ramekins in plastic wrap and place in the refrigerator for at least 2 hours, or overnight to completely chill.

To serve, run a thin-bladed knife around the edges of the *flan*, and then invert the ramekin onto a serving plate. If you find that the *flan* is sticking to the ramekin, dip the bottom of the ramekin into a bowl of hot water for 1–2 minutes.

CREAMY LECHE FLAN CUSTARD

A standard, and beloved, Filipino dessert, *leche flan* is a sweet caramel custard usually made from canned condensed milk and canned evaporated milk. The dish is a great example of how Filipinos have been able to adapt and transform seemingly simple canned goods into something so decadent. *Leche flan* can range in texture from extremely heavy and dense to creamy and light. In fact, my grandmother often uses a dozen egg yolks alone in her very rich *leche flan*. After much experimentation, though, I've found that using 2 large eggs and 4 large egg yolks strikes the right balance for a rich and creamy *flan* that isn't overly dense. Mine is a simple and straightforward recipe for *leche flan* that results in an amazingly smooth and creamy dessert.

RESOURCE GUIDE

Here are a few online sources that will help you track down certain harder-to-find ingredients.

Caw Caw Creek
Website: *cawcawcreek.com*
Grower and supplier of heritage pasture-raised pork products (belly, jowl, and ears).

Eighth Wonder Rice
Website: *heirloomrice.com*
Importer and supplier of a number of heirloom rice varieties grown in the Philippines.

Four Winds Growers
Website: *fourwindsgrowers.com*
Online supplier of potted citrus trees, including *calamansi*.

Kalustyan's
Website: *kalustyans.com*
Provides a selection of ethnic spices and specialty food products.

Melissa's Produce
Website: *melissas.com*
The largest distributor of specialty produce in the U.S.

Penzey's Spices
Website: *penzeys.com*
Provides a wide selection of spices, salts, herbs, and dried chili peppers.

PhilAmFood
Website: *philamfood.com*
Online Filipino food and grocery store.

VuQo
Website: *vuqo.com*
Premium vodka distilled from Philippine coconut nectar.

Xroads Philippines Sea Salts
Website: *philippineseasalts.com*
Purveyors of premium gourmet Filipino sea salts.

BIBLIOGRAPHY

In conducting the research necessary for this cookbook, I relied upon a number of sources that were not only informative, but inspirational as well. The most enjoyable part of this research was discovering Filipino culinary and cultural history in places I least expected to find them. The authors of these books all served as teachers and mentors to me through their words and pages.

Alegre, Edilberto N. and Fernandez, Doreen G. *Kinilaw: A Philippine Cuisine of Freshness*. Manila: Bookmark Publishing, 1991

Alejandro, Reynaldo Gamboa and Reyes-Lumen, Nancy. *The Adobo Book*. Manila: Anvil Publishing, 2004

Aranas, Jennifer. *The Filipino-American Kitchen*. Vermont: Tuttle Publishing, 2006

Baker Jr., Charles H. *Jigger, Beaker, and Glass: Drinking Around the World*. Lanham, MD: The Derrydale Press, 1992 Originally published as: *Gentleman's Companion Vol. 2*. 1939

Baretto, Glenda Rosales, et al. *Kulinarya: A Guidebook to Philippine Cuisine*. Manila: Anvil Publishing, 2008

Berry, Jeff and Kaye, Annene. *Grog Log*. Canada: Dan Vado Publishing, 1998

Berry, Jeff. *Sippin' Safari*. San Jose: Club Tiki Press, 2007

Besa, Amy and Dorotan, Romy. *Memories of Philippine Kitchens*. New York: Stewart Tabori & Chang, 2006

Brown, Alton. *I'm Just Here For More Food*. New York: Steward Tabori & Chang, 2004

Fernandez, Doreen G. *Tikim: Essays on Philippine Food and Culture*. Manila: Anvil Publishing, 1994

McGee, Harold. *On Food and Cooking: The Science and Lore of the Kitchen*. New York: Scribner, 2004

Nguyen, Andrea. *Asian Dumplings: Mastering Gyoza, Spring Rolls, Samosas, and More*. Berkeley: Ten Speed Press, 2009

Santa Maria, Felice. *The Governor-General's Kitchen: Philippine Culinary Vignettes and Period Recipes, 1521–1935*. Manila: Anvil Publishing, 2006

Tayag, Claude and Quioc, Mary Ann. *Linamnam: Eating One's Way Around the Philippines*. Manila: Anvil Publishing, 2012

PHOTOGRAPHY IN THIS BOOK

Before writing this cookbook, the only camera I owned was of the simple point-and-shoot variety. So when I decided that I was also going to do all of the food styling and food photography for this book (in addition to all the writing and recipe developing), I figured I should probably upgrade my camera. I also figured that I was going to have a very long and difficult road ahead of me. I figured right. Soon, a shiny brand new Canon EOS Rebel T3i DSLR camera arrived on my doorstep along with a 50mm f/1.4 lens. "Cool," I thought, "Look at all those random letters and numbers on the boxes. They all probably mean that I'm going to take some awesome pictures." I by no means ever assumed that taking my own pictures for my cookbook was going to be easy—I had way too much respect for all the food bloggers and food photographers who work extremely hard at what they do. But I couldn't help but feel giddy once my new camera arrived.

Trouble was, I had no idea how to work the thing. Luckily, my younger brother Darren, an avid photographer and wielder of heavy cameras, was around to help. He even loaned me his fancy-pants Canon 50D along with a 50mm macro f/2.5 lens (more random letters and numbers!). I ended up shooting a majority of the pictures for this cookbook on my own camera using both lenses, and a handful of other pictures on my brother's camera using both lenses.

Ultimately though, having the luxury of two cameras and two lenses was more than I could handle. I would frantically email, text or call my little brother with inane questions like, "How am I supposed to see anything through this tiny peephole?" or, "Why would I want to auto-focus in manual mode? It's called MANUAL mode!" and

"Why the @#$% isn't my tether option working!!!" Once I got the cameras figured out, I still had to wrestle with the fact that, aside from the simple pictures from my blog, I had no experience whatsoever styling food. I spent some of the most frustrating hours of my life standing behind my camera(s), driving myself crazy when I couldn't get a garlic clove to lean just so, or when a singular *pancit* noodle zigged when I wanted it to zag, or all the times I thought I had the perfect picture only to find a smudge or a drip where there shouldn't have been a smudge or a drip.

There were many times when I wanted to give up and have my two-year-old son just doodle some pictures for me—surely the doodles would have been better than what I was shooting. But then I realized that, like my son's artwork, my pictures didn't have to be perfect. I realized that Filipino food is already full of colors and textures; it's already visually stunning without having to be staged or overly styled. So with this new mindset, I became more at ease with photographing my recipes. And soon, the food started to come alive for me. I styled and photographed all of the food photographs in this cookbook. All were shot under natural light, either in my living room next to a big sliding glass door, or in my kitchen near a couple of windows. All are 100% real—no fake food, stand-ins or other such trickery. As for the photographs of my grandmother and me, those are courtesy of my little brother. After I completed the manuscript and photos for this cookbook, I gained deeper appreciation for the beauty of Filipino food—not only through the recipes, but through the photographs as well.

Unfortunately, one of the most troubling myths about Filipino food is that it is all brown, greasy and visually unappealing. But as you flip through the pages of this cookbook, I hope that you'll see Filipino food in the same light that I do. Filipino food, in all its simplicity, is naturally beautiful.

ACKNOWLEDGMENTS

While 20.. was a year of great joy for me, it was also a year fraught with sadness. It was the year in which I was blessed to sign a contract with Tuttle Publishing for the cookbook you see here. And it was the year in which I was able to happily walk away from my successful and pioneering food truck, The Manila Machine.

Despite these joyous events, that year started with the sad news of my maternal grandfather, Gregorio Ladera, passing away in the Philippines in January. When I was very young, my Grandpa Guyo lived with us in the States and practically raised me and my brothers while my parents worked long hours. Because of my Grandpa Guyo's influence, I learned to find contentment in the simplest of things. And for that, I am thankful. I'll always remember his love of *pancit* noodles.

Just a few short weeks after my Grandpa Guyo's passing, I learned that my paternal grandfather, Juan Gapultos, had fallen ill and perhaps did not have much longer to be with his family. Although I had previously decided to end my food truck business to spend more time with my wife and son and to focus on this cookbook, the news of my Grandpa Johnny's health made my decision that much easier. I now had the luxury to spend time with my family and to visit with my Grandpa Johnny on most weekends until he finally passed away in August of that year. My Grandpa Johnny taught me many things in life, but chief among them was a love of family. And for that I am thankful. I'll always remember his love of the bitter Filipino soup; *papaitan*.

I am forever grateful for the guidance my grandfathers provided me throughout my life—without that guidance, this cookbook would not have been possible. I am also fortunate to have a close circle of family and friends who have helped to make this cookbook possible. This cookbook truly is a longtime dream come true for me.

First and foremost, I'd like to thank my grandmother, Estrella Gapultos (AKA Grandma Esther). Thank you for instilling in me a love for our food and our culture.

Thank you to my Great Aunties—AKA Grandma Carling and Grandma Puyong—for keeping it real. Your *miki* and *pinakbet* are unrivaled and unequaled.

Thank you to my wonderfully supportive, loving and understanding wife, Barbara. No matter how zany and crazy an idea I've had, you've always been there to push me forward to reach my goals. Thank you for keeping our household in order while I was toiling away on a food truck. You are an incredible wife and mother.

To my son, Bruce. One day it'll all make sense.

To my parents, Mario and Clarita Gapultos. You are the first to doubt, but I always get the last laugh. Thanks for keeping me fed all these years.

My older brother, Claudell, tested a few of the recipes in this book and provided some very positive feedback when I was expecting a punch to the stomach. He also let me raid his cupboards for a few pieces of dishware that I used as props in some of the photos in this book (I got tired of buying and returning dishes to certain housewares stores). Thanks big brother!

My little brother, Darren, a wielder of heavy cameras and deep sighs, provided me with much needed photography and computer advice during the creation of this cookbook. He also loaned me his fancy-pants camera and lens that I used for a handful of photos throughout this cookbook. And he's also responsible for photographing my snazzy headshot on the back flap of this book. Thanks, little brother!

My cousin Kathy Fermin perhaps has the best palate and taste buds of anyone I know. I learned a lot about balancing flavors from her. Thank you Kathy for recipe testing, and thanks for double-checking my Tagalog!

Thank you to the entire team at Tuttle Publishing for giving me the wonderful opportunity to share a part of my culture with the rest of the world. Thank you to William Notte for recognizing the potential in my proposal. And thank you also to Rowan Muelling-Auer, Gail Tok, and Christopher Johns. My gratitude also goes to Jon Steever, June Chong, and Irene Ho for making sense out of my words and images and transforming them into a great cookbook.

Many thanks to Norman Kolpas at UCLA. You read the very first draft of my cookbook proposal, and instead of throwing it in the trash, you encouraged me to pursue my dreams of writing this cookbook. Thank you for finding the promise and spark in that proposal.

The title of this cookbook is due in large part to Amy Scattergood of LA Weekly. Back in 2011, Amy wrote a very nice story about me entitled "Adobo Road." The team at Tuttle liked that article title so much, that we decided to use it as part of the title for this cookbook. Thankfully, Amy gave me her blessing to use the title. Thanks again Amy, and thanks for doing what you can to promote Filipino food.

Nerissa Silao went above and beyond in her efforts to help promote this cookbook. Thank you so much for spreading the word and for helping me toot my own horn when you thought I was being much too timid!

My friend, Cameron Rhudy, gave me a kick in the pants to start a food blog oh so many years ago. Thanks for those words of encouragement. And thanks for all the free legal advice I needed to navigate my food truck.

Thank you Nastassia Johnson for partnering with me on The Manila Machine.

Thank you to my Friend of Friends, Matt Hurst. Your positive attitude and your attempts at levity during stressful times were greatly appreciated—even though I hardly ever laughed. Drinks soon.

Thank you to Bee Yin Low, for all the camera and cookbook writing advice you gave me.

Thank you to blogger and author extraordinaire, Jaden Hair, for opening the door for me at Tuttle and for all the blogger/business advice you gave me in the past.

Many, many thanks to Pat Tanumihardja. You've helped me in so many ways over the last few years that I really don't know where to begin. Thank you for all your help with my proposal and thank you so much for always being so candid and honest with all of your advice.

Thank you Andrea Nguyen for always taking the time to answer the glut of questions I always seemed to have for you. Your advice, words of wisdom and encouragement meant so much to me. You are truly an inspiration.

When I first started my food truck, cookbook author and restaurateur Amy Besa reached out to me and offered some honest advice and well wishes. Since that time, Amy has continued to be nothing but helpful and supportive of my efforts in promoting Filipino food. Thank you, Amy.

To Claude Tayag. Thank you for fighting the good fight and for being the keeper of the Filipino culinary flame. You're a great role model for all of us. *Salamat*.

I also would like to thank the readers of Burnt Lumpia. Honestly and truly, this cookbook would not be possible without you. I couldn't have gotten to this point without making the connections I've made with all of you. Thank you for supporting me and Filipino food all these years!

And lastly, I want to give a big thanks to all the recipe testers that helped make this cookbook what it is. The following people provided the brutally honest feedback I needed by volunteering their time, and their discerning palates, to test each recipe in this cookbook:

Janice Agagas
Darlene Arriola
Niya Bajaj
Johanna Blanco
Rhea Borja
Fred Briones
Reynila Calderon-Magbuhat
Kathy Chan
Melissa Coulson
Allison Day
Kathy Fermin
Ann Frosch
Claudell Gapultos
Darren Gapultos
Vanilynne Gulla
Marilou Guy
Cheryl Harmon
Vicky Haworth
Katie Hillman & Louie Aragon
Matt and Suzanne Hurst
Honnie Aguilar Leinartas
Alfredo Lopez
Remil Mangali
Gio Ray T. Mangaya-ay
Roland & Patricia Miranda
Marina Mont'Ros
Heather Neal
Vince Nievares
Marie Oria
Cathy Pascual
Tracey Paska
Magida Perez-Najjar
Malou Perez-Nievera
Shannon Petersen
Jason Plurad
William Pilz
Elizabeth Besa Quirino
Sally-Rose Salcedo
Emily Salvani
Dudut Santiago
Paul Selkirk
Leslie Scheil
Alfred Sta. Iglesia
Allison Stearns
Randi Tanakaya
Pat Tanumihardja
Tshilaba Verite
Scott D. Webster
Gina Dalisay Wong

DEDICATION

For my grandfathers: Gentle men, big appetites.

Gregorio Ladera
November 24, 1914—January 11, 2011

Juan Martín Gapultos
June 12, 1928—August 3, 2011

INDEX

Published by Tuttle Publishing, an imprint of
Periplus Editions (HK) Ltd.

www.tuttlepublishing.com

LCCN 2012042004

ISBN: 978-0-8048-4257-0

Distributed by
North America, Latin America & Europe
Tuttle Publishing
364 Innovation Drive
North Clarendon, VT 05759-9436 U.S.A.
Tel: (802) 773-8930; Fax: (802) 773-6993
info@tuttlepublishing.com
www.tuttlepublishing.com

Japan
Tuttle Publishing
Yaekari Building
3rd Floor, 5-4-12 Osaki
Shinagawa-ku
Tokyo 141-0032
Tel: (81) 3 5437-0171; Fax: (81) 3 5437-0755
sales@tuttle.co.jp
www.tuttle.co.jp

Asia Pacific
Berkeley Books Pte. Ltd.
3 Kallang Sector #04-01,
Singapore 349278
Tel: (65) 6741 2178; Fax: (65) 6741 2179
inquiries@periplus.com.sg
www.tuttlepublishing.com

23 22 21 20 19
10 9 8 7 6 5 4

Printed in Hong Kong   1906EP

TUTTLE PUBLISHING® is a registered trademark of
Tuttle Publishing, a division of Periplus Editions (HK) Ltd.

ABOUT TUTTLE: "BOOKS TO SPAN THE EAST AND WEST"

Our core mission at Tuttle Publishing is to create books which bring people together one page at a time. Tuttle was
founded in 1832 in the small New England town of Rutland, Vermont (USA). Our fundamental values remain as
strong today as they were then—to publish best-in-class books informing the English-speaking world about the
countries and peoples of Asia. The world has become a smaller place today and Asia's economic, cultural and
political influence has expanded, yet the need for meaningful dialogue and information about this diverse region
has never been greater. Since 1948, Tuttle has been a leader in publishing books on the cultures, arts, cuisines,
languages and literatures of Asia. Our authors and photographers have won numerous awards and Tuttle has
published thousands of books on subjects ranging from martial arts to paper crafts. We welcome you to explore
the wealth of information available on Asia at **www.tuttlepublishing.com**.